Bonhoeffer for Armchair Theologians

Also Available in the Armchair Series

# Bonhoeffer
# for Armchair Theologians

STEPHEN R. HAYNES
LORI BRANDT HALE

ILLUSTRATIONS BY RON HILL

WJK WESTMINSTER
JOHN KNOX PRESS
LOUISVILLE · KENTUCKY

*1st edition*
Published by Westminster John Knox Press
Louisville, Kentucky

09 10 11 12 13 14 15 16 17 18—10 9 8 7 6 5 4 3 2 1

*Book design by Sharon Adams*
*Cover design by Jennifer K. Cox*
*Cover illustration by Ron Hill*

**Library of Congress Cataloging-in-Publication Data**

Haynes, Stephen R.
  Bonhoeffer for armchair theologians / Stephen R. Haynes, Lori Brandt
Hale. — 1st ed.
    p. cm. — (Armchair series)
  Includes bibliographical references (p.      ) and index.
  ISBN 978-0-664-23010-4 (alk. paper)
  1. Bonhoeffer, Dietrich, 1906–1945. I. Hale, Lori Brandt. II. Title.
BX4827.B57H36 2009
230'.044092—dc22

                                        2009011993

PRINTED IN THE UNITED STATES OF AMERICA

♾ The paper used in this publication meets the minimum require-
ments of the American National Standard for Information
Sciences—Permanence of Paper for Printed Library Materials,
ANSI Z39.48-1992

Westminster John Knox Press advocates the responsible use
of our natural resources. The text paper of this book is made
from 30% post-consumer waste.

# Contents

# CHAPTER ONE

## Life

Many recountings of Bonhoeffer's biography begin at the end, suggesting that the meaning of his life can only be comprehended by looking backward from his anti-Nazi resistance, imprisonment, and execution. But we will attempt to view Bonhoeffer's life as it was lived—from beginning to end. It started in a relatively idyllic time when terms such as "world war," "fascism," and "genocide" were not yet part of the European lexicon.

## Family Background

Bonhoeffer's family bequeathed to him a proud heritage. In addition to a concrete inheritance that included the writings of Luther and Schleiermacher and a signet ring with the Bonhoeffer family's sixteenth-century coat of arms, Dietrich's ancestors—the Bonhoeffers, von Hases, and Kalckreuths—left to him a keen intellect, an impressive musical aptitude, and a comfort in his own skin.

His great-grandfather Karl August von Hase was a professor of church and dogmatic history called by Johann Wolfgang von Goethe to the University in Jena. Karl August's son Karl Alfred—Dietrich's maternal grandfather—was chaplain to Wilhelm II of Prussia. His son Hans von Hase—Dietrich's uncle—was a rural pastor. On his father's side, Bonhoeffer's ancestors included respectable government officials, as well as socialists, Freemasons, and Swedenborgians. Dietrich's paternal grandmother was Julie Tafel Bonhoeffer, a forceful woman whose independence and progressive thinking impressed the young man. He lived in her home during his first year of university studies.

Dietrich's father, Karl Bonhoeffer, was a psychiatrist who began his professional career in 1893 in the Silesian city of Breslau (now Wroclaw in Poland), which had over 400,000 inhabitants at the turn of the twentieth century. Three years later Karl met Dietrich's mother, Paula von Hase, whose father had recently become a church official and professor in the city. They were married in 1898 and began a family the following year. Eight children were born to the couple over the next decade, including the twins Dietrich and Sabine in 1906. The Bonhoeffers lived in a spacious house with half a dozen servants and at least as many pets; soon there was a summer home in the Harz Mountains as well. The children received their early education from their mother, who often accompanied Dietrich to worship despite the fact that the Bonhoeffers were not regular churchgoers.

## Childhood and Studies

In 1912 the family moved to Berlin, where Karl Bonhoeffer had been appointed head of the psychiatric department at the prestigious Charité Hospital. The following year Dietrich began attending gymnasium (a humanities-oriented German secondary school that prepares students for university education). In addition to excelling in the humanistic disciplines, Dietrich became an accomplished pianist and was playing Mozart sonatas by the age of ten. In 1916 the family moved to a house on Wangenheimstrasse in the upper-middle-class district of Grunewald.

In 1917 Dietrich's older brothers Karl-Friedrich and Walter were called up for military duty; within two weeks Walter was dead from shrapnel wounds sustained while marching to the front. The twelve-year-old Dietrich received his brother's confirmation Bible and an abiding appreciation for the human cost of war. At age thirteen Bonhoeffer began attending the Grunewald Gymnasium (now Walter-Rathenau Gymnasium), from which one could hear the gunfire exchanged by communists and defenders of the fledgling Weimar Republic. Dietrich was a successful though not stellar student. His certificate of completion indicated a young man "very good" in behavior, "good" in religion, "sufficient" in English, and "insufficient" in handwriting.

## You Want to Study What?

Dietrich was blessed (and cursed?) to be born into a family of successful men. By the time he began to chart a direction

in life, his older brother Karl-Friedrich (b. 1899) was on his way to becoming a world-renowned physicist; before his untimely death Walter (1899–1918) had demonstrated great linguistic facility; and Klaus (b. 1901) was an accomplished cello player and promising law student. The boys' father, furthermore, occupied the country's leading professorship in psychiatry and neurology. How would the young Dietrich deal with the pressure to succeed in such a household? By setting into territory that was uncharted by Bonhoeffers of his generation.

Despite early signs of piety and the prominence of ancestors who had been pastors and theologians, it was a shock when Dietrich announced at age thirteen that he would study theology. According to Eberhard Bethge, his siblings "tried to convince him that he was taking the path of least resistance, and that the church to which he proposed to devote himself was a poor, feeble, boring, petty and bourgeois institution." Undeterred, Bonhoeffer reportedly responded, "In that case I shall reform it!"[1] For their part, his parents feared that their son would have to endure an "uneventful pastor's life" while missing his true vocation—which they assumed was music. Yet Dietrich was firm in his resolve. While still at gymnasium he studied Hebrew and read Friedrich Schleiermacher, the father of "liberal" Protestant theology. Nevertheless, Dietrich would remain suspended for some time between theological study as a "science" (that is, a branch of knowledge) and service to the church.

## Tübingen, Rome, Berlin

If Dietrich's choice of subject matter was surprising, his choice of a university was not. In the fall of 1923, amid political instability and hyperinflation, he followed family tradition and enrolled at Tübingen University. Dietrich's academic work during his two semesters at Tübingen encompassed logic, epistemology, music, political science, and history of religions, in addition to biblical, church historical, and dogmatic subjects. Yet he still had time to join the Hedgehog fraternity of which his father and uncle had been members, and spend fourteen days in military training. Bonhoeffer felt obligated to "perform one's duty for two weeks" in case it became necessary to protect the republic from radical forces. It was the only time Bonhoeffer would ever be a soldier.

By late 1923 hyperinflation had made living away from home a burden on Bonhoeffer's family. (In August he wrote his parents requesting "an additional 10 million" marks to buy food; a few weeks later he reported that "each meal costs 10 billion"). But before returning to Berlin, Dietrich convinced his parents to let him spend a term in Rome, where, he reassured them, study would be "much less expensive." In April he and brother Klaus crossed the Alps and began what Bonhoeffer later called "a quarter of special studies." The main focus of these studies turned out to be exploration. The brothers visited Bologna, Florence, Siena, Pompeii, Milan, and Sicily. In Libya, to which they sailed amid a "colorful throng . . . [of] military personnel, immigrants, Turks and Arabs,"[2] the Bonhoeffers encountered Islamic culture.

More than anywhere he visited, though, the young Bonhoeffer became enthralled by Catholic Rome, particularly

the way it symbolized the church as a tangible, universal entity with ancient roots. On Palm Sunday 1924 Dietrich attended mass in St. Peter's, where he would return several times during Holy Week. During a second sojourn in Rome, Bonhoeffer even had an audience with the pope. In June 1924 he finally returned to Berlin and enrolled at Friedrich Wilhelm (later Humboldt) University, where he would remain a student until July 1927.

Bonhoeffer's main professor at Berlin was theologian Reinhold Seeberg, whose work on the history of Christian doctrine became a medium for Bonhoeffer's knowledge of the classical theologians, particularly Luther. Furthermore, Seeberg's emphasis on the social dimension of human existence contributed to a growing sensitivity to "sociality" in Bonhoeffer's thought. Under Seeberg, Bonhoeffer began his dissertation at the end of 1925 at the age of nineteen and completed it in eighteen months. (If you have ever been a graduate student, you will probably need to read that sentence again.) After considering other topics, Bonhoeffer decided to work in the area of ecclesiology (a subfield of theology concerned with the nature of the church). In *Sanctorum Communio: A Dogmatic Inquiry into the Sociology of the Church* he brought together social philosophy and the (Barthian) theology of revelation and introduced a "theology of sociality" built on a relational view of personhood. Revelation in its social form—the church—was described as "Christ existing as community." Seeberg called it "a very satisfactory model of serious academic erudition."[3]

Despite the fact that Seeberg taught Dietrich in seven classes and directed his dissertation, they were not kindred theological spirits. Seeberg represented a Protestant liberalism that was devoted to harmonizing "the Bible and the modern spirit, Luther and idealism, theology and philosophy."[4] In a 1930 letter, Bonhoeffer offered an assessment of this harmonizing impulse when he described one of Seeberg's sermons as "shallow religious babble for forty-five minutes."[5] Increasingly, Bonhoeffer believed that the anthropological optimism of this tradition was poorly suited to the cultural and theological crises that faced European society.

## Liberation: Part One

Under Seeberg, Adolf von Harnack, and Luther scholar Karl Holl, Bonhoeffer encountered the thinkers who would shape his own thought. These included Augustine, Aquinas, and Schleiermacher on the theological side, and Kant, Hegel, Nietzsche, Heidegger, and Dilthey among the philosophers. But without doubt, Bonhoeffer's two greatest intellectual influences were to be Martin Luther and Karl Barth.

From Luther, Bonhoeffer took a thoroughgoing emphasis on justification by faith (whose relationship to obedience he explored in his book *Discipleship*), as well as a *theologia crucis* ("theology of the cross") which nurtured his conviction that God's presence is paradoxically revealed in weakness and suffering. Luther's centrality to Bonhoeffer's thought is hardly surprising given Dietrich's identity as a German Protestant who came of age during the Luther Renaissance of the 1920s and studied under Holl, the leading Luther scholar of his generation.

Less predictable in the development of the young Berlin theologian was the role of Karl Barth (1886–1968), the Swiss pastor-turned-theologian who announced the bankruptcy of Protestant liberalism and proffered a theology of revelation whose starting point was not human religious experience but the word of a wholly other God. Barth

assailed the theological establishment in part by drawing attention to the vapidity of liberal optimism in a Europe devastated by war. "One can *not* speak of God simply by speaking of man in a loud voice,"[6] Barth wrote in an observation that was characteristically both clever and penetrating. He was speaking of Schleiermacher, but he had in mind the tradition of cultural Protestantism that had dominated the universities, the Protestant church leadership, and German culture since the end of the nineteenth century.

After his first semester in Berlin, Bonhoeffer was busily reading Max Weber, Ernst Troeltsch, and Edmund Husserl, scholars whose ideas were then being appropriated by academic theologians. Around the same time he encountered Barth, a writer conspicuously absent from the reading lists of his Berlin professors. At the end of 1924 Dietrich discovered Barth's *The Epistle to the Romans* (2nd ed., 1922) and *The Word of God and the Word of Man* (1924) and obtained notes from lectures Barth would publish as *Prologomena to Christian Dogmatics* in 1927. This encounter with Barth's theology was "like a liberation," according to Bonhoeffer. Among other things, it determined the sorts of questions that interested him. Dietrich's first student paper in systematic theology, written during the summer of 1925, explored whether one can "distinguish between a historical and a pneumatological [spiritual] interpretation of Scripture"—a question thrust before the attention of continental theologians by the success of Barth's *Epistle to the Romans.* In this paper Bonhoeffer sought to pass beyond the historical-critical studies that guided academic biblical interpretation to a place where humans enter what Barth called the "strange new world of the Bible."

The impact of Barth's "dialectical theology" (so called because the infinite distance between the human and the divine means that our knowledge of God is paradoxical in character) became more evident after Bonhoeffer left Berlin. In 1928 he offered a Barthian assessment of "religion" as sinful self-justification, the antithesis of "faith." "Religion and morality," he wrote in a sentence that could have come from *Epistle to the Romans*, "is the most dangerous enemy of the Christian message of good news."[7] At Union Theological Seminary in New York in 1930 Bonhoeffer became known as an apologist for Barth's "theology of crisis" (another term for dialectical theology). And when he lectured on the history of twentieth-century systematic theology at Berlin in early 1932, Bonhoeffer offered a detailed presentation of the Barthian "revolution" in which the object of theology is the revealed Word, and God is no longer confused with religion.[8]

Yet Bonhoeffer always remained a critical Barthian. In his dissertations of 1927 and 1929 he carried on a conversation with Barth regarding "the problems of ethics"; specifically, Bonhoeffer wondered whether Barth's conviction that no finite historical moment was *capax infiniti* (capable of the infinite) ruled out concrete ethics and proclamation since, as Bonhoeffer read Barth, "empirical human activity—be it faith, obedience—is at best a reference to God's activity and in its historicity can never be faith and obedience itself."[9] Despite such lingering questions, there is no doubt that Bonhoeffer's discovery of Barth represented his first great liberation from the thinking of his Berlin professors and infused his academic work with a newfound joy.

The two men's personal relationship began after Bonhoeffer's return from America in July 1931. Traveling to Bonn, Bonhoeffer anonymously attended a 7 a.m. lecture (where he heard some of what would become *Church*

*Dogmatics* vol. 1, part 1), caught Barth's attention with a timely quotation from Luther, and was invited to the professor's home for dinner and conversation. Barth was impressed with the twenty-five-year-old theologian, and the two met and corresponded regularly over the ensuing years.

Barth may have become Bonhoeffer's most important theological mentor, but their relationship was not immune to tension or misunderstanding. This was particularly true in 1933 when Bonhoeffer left for London at the height of the German church struggle without consulting his older colleague. In a scolding letter, Barth wrote, "You were

quite right not to seek any wisdom from me before [leaving]. I would have advised against it, unconditionally and certainly bringing up the heaviest artillery I could muster." He added (though it probably wasn't necessary), "Just be glad I don't have you here in front of me." Barth assured Bonhoeffer that if he did not matter so much to him he would not have taken him "by the collar in this fashion," but it must have been a stinging tongue-lashing nonetheless.[10]

Although Bonhoeffer was often referred to "a follower" of Barth, it is more accurate to see him as charting his own course in the charged space between liberalism and dialectical theology. The contentious relationship between the liberal establishment and the upstart crisis theology was on display in a public exchange of letters between Barth and Adolf von Harnack during 1923. Since both men exercised considerable influence on the young theologian, the testy Barth-Harnack correspondence reflects the tensions in Bonhoeffer's own theological development. These tensions were on display in a classroom discussion of Barth's theology in which Bonhoeffer contradicted Harnack "politely, but on objective theological grounds," and in Harnack's warning to Bonhoeffer about the threat posed by "contempt for academic theology and by unscholarly theologies."[11]

## Lectern or Pulpit?

Barth's theology of revelation affected not only the content of Bonhoeffer's thought but his approach to theology as well. According to Eberhard Bethge, "The distinctive task of preaching—the earthly, concrete proof of God's word in the words repeated by human beings—was the starting point for this new theology, and this tore him away from the game of speculation."[12] Among the human words that interested Bonhoeffer were those employed in the church's training of children. The most difficult theological pronouncements, Bonhoeffer wrote at the time, were worthless if they could not be explained to children. Thus in late 1926, as he initiated work on his dissertation, Bonhoeffer began giving regular children's "meditations" at his church in Grunewald. Out of this experience grew the "Thursday Circle," a regular reading and discussion evening for older youth held in Bonhoeffer's home.

A month after his dissertation was accepted by the Berlin faculty in December 1927, Bonhoeffer took the first theological examination required for pastors. Although he earned a grade of only "sufficient" and his sermon was criticized for "pomposity, exaggeration, and clumsiness," Bonhoeffer's interest in the ministry was not diminished. To test the pastoral waters he sought a position as a church vicar (or pastoral intern). Some in Berlin advised him not to break ties with his parish in Grunewald or with the university's theological faculty. But in February 1928 Dietrich

was off to Barcelona, where he would serve as pastor-in-training to a congregation of three hundred German businessmen and their families. He traveled to Spain via Paris, from which he wrote prophetically that the Tauentzien-strasse, a working-class neighborhood in Berlin, would be "an extremely fruitful field for church work."[13] Bonhoeffer was to find the social contrasts of the German capital even starker in Barcelona.

Bonhoeffer's year in Spain brought him freedom to travel, and he used it to once again explore North Africa. Among the memorable Spanish experiences enjoyed by the twenty-two-year-old German were the bullfight and the purchase of a painting he believed to be a Picasso. As a site for pastoral training, however, Barcelona was of limited usefulness, because the resident pastor was concerned mainly with performing the standard parish duties. Seeking to build on his past achievements in the area of youth work, Dietrich developed a successful children's Sunday school (with an average attendance of forty) and produced a Nativity play that was performed "to great satisfaction." He was also keen to arrange for religious instruction at the local secondary school but had to settle for a discussion group that met in private homes. Bonhoeffer's supervisor, Fritz Olbricht, praised both his "sensitive, charming nature" and his way with the colony's young people, who were "enthusiastically devoted to him."[14]

Despite Olbricht's appreciation for his vicar's "competency in every respect," Bonhoeffer reported that not once during his year in Spain had he and the supervising minister discussed "a theological, let alone a religious question."[15] But Olbricht did allow Dietrich to write and deliver nineteen sermons over the course of the year, and this forced him to give this "precious half hour" the attention it deserved. In his Barcelona sermons Bonhoeffer was

most confident when speaking of the gospel as if telling children "a fairy tale about a foreign country."[16]

During his foreign sojourn, Bonhoeffer exercised his academic muscles by revising his dissertation for publication and writing a series of lectures such as "The Tragedy of Prophecy and Its Lasting Meaning" and "Jesus Christ and the Essence of Christianity." These evening talks contained seeds that would come to fruition in Bonhoeffer's mature theology, such as "Christ is not the bringer of a new religion, but the bringer of God."[17] Yet they also contained the occasional weed that would have to be extirpated. For instance, in his lecture "Basic Questions of a Christian Ethic" (February 1929) Bonhoeffer defended war on the basis of a sacred obligation to the members of one's *Volk* (in German the word connotes both "people" and "race"). Bonhoeffer never again wrote so cavalierly of war and its moral justification; in fact, his writing and speaking during the 1930s is conspicuous for its prioritizing of peace, an extremely unpopular position in interwar Germany, where pacifism, internationalism, and even ecumenism were regarded with suspicion and contempt. But it is important to note that despite Bonhoeffer's early and steadfast opposition to Nazism, he was not immune to the *völkisch* thinking (an intellectual movement growing out of nineteenth-century romantic nationalism that emphasized the bonds of ethnicity) that was so common in post–World War I Germany.

His year in Barcelona did not lead Bonhoeffer to forsake academic life for the church or to abandon the pulpit for the lecture hall. He decided to engage in postdoctoral work upon returning to Berlin but was still undecided about whether to pursue an academic or pastoral career.

## Berlin Again, and New York

In the months after Dietrich returned to Berlin in February 1929 the foundations of the Weimar Republic were being shaken by economic hardship and the electoral success of the National Socialists. Although Bonhoeffer's resistance to the growing German nationalism was indicated by his occasional presence at the church of notorious pacifist Günther Dehn, he did not become directly engaged in politics. Rather, he threw himself into his work, specifically completion of the postdoctoral thesis (*Habilitationsschrift*) required for an academic career, duties associated with his position as a teaching assistant (without compensation) in Berlin's department of systematic theology, and youth work in his Grunewald congregation.

The second dissertation, titled *Act and Being: Transcendental Philosophy and Ontology in Systematic Theology,* was a study in theological anthropology. As in *Sanctorum Communio,* Bonhoeffer placed modern and contemporary thinkers into dialogue with one another and with theologians. Here Barth and Rudolf Bultmann (1884–1976) were addressed, as well as Hegel and Heidegger. While most readers find these books far less accessible than *Discipleship* or *Ethics,* they are important for understanding Bonhoeffer's mature theology. In July 1930 Bonhoeffer delivered his inaugural lecture, "The Anthropological Question in Contemporary Philosophy and Theology," which explored the theological anthropology under development in his dissertations.

Meanwhile Bonhoeffer had not relinquished the idea of a church vocation. The same month of his inaugural lecture he took the second round of church examinations necessary for pastoral ordination and completed the required sermon and catechesis. The latter revealed once again Bonhoeffer's talent for reaching young people. One evaluator of his catechesis commented on the candidate's ability to "rivet the attention of the children and to prompt them to participate on their own."[18] Impressed with Bonhoeffer's potential as a pastor to youth, Church General Superintendent Max Diestel promised to keep him in mind for a student chaplaincy at the technical college in Charlottenburg. Yet because Bonhoeffer was not old enough for ordination, Diestel suggested he travel to America while "still young." It did not take much encouragement to send Dietrich overseas again. Reflecting on the multiple talents of his young charge, Diestel noted in his recommendation

NEW YORK, NEW YORK!

that Bonhoeffer's "academic training to this point has been very good, although his practical skills (sermon, catechesis, etc.) should not be underestimated either."[19]

In the wake of the Wall Street crash, Bonhoeffer arrived in New York to spend a year as a Sloane Fellow at Union Theological Seminary in Upper Manhattan. In 1930 Union was the flagship of American divinity schools, its faculty boasting such prominent figures as Reinhold Niebuhr, John Baillie, and Harry Emerson Fosdick. Yet the curriculum struck Bonhoeffer as soft. Instead of the dogmatic and exegetical subjects to which he was accustomed, Dietrich found courses with titles like "Church and Community: The Cooperation of the Church with Social and Character-Building Agencies," "Ethical Issues in the Social Order," and "The Minister's Work with Individuals."

In a mid-year report to Diestel, Bonhoeffer complained that "there is no theology here. . . . They talk a blue streak without the slightest substantive foundation." The seminarians, he wrote, are "completely clueless" about dogmatics and "intoxicated with liberal and humanistic phrases," while in the churches the sermon has been "reduced to parenthetical church remarks about newspaper events."[20] In spite of, or perhaps because of, these judgments, Dietrich reported being drawn more and more to the ministry. While he did not do much preaching, he became deeply involved in church work.

If Bonhoeffer was ambivalent about learning from Americans, he was much in demand as a lecturer on the situation in Germany and the prospects for another war. While refusing to ignore the suffering brought on Germany by the Great War or the effects of the Versailles Treaty's insistence on German "war guilt," Bonhoeffer emphasized the burgeoning aspirations for peace in his homeland. He also became an ambassador for the dialectical theology that had yet to catch on in America. He lectured on Barth in the systematic theology seminar of John Baillie, who later described Bonhoeffer as "the most convinced disciple of Dr. Barth that had appeared among us [at Union] up to that time, and withal as stout an opponent of liberalism as had ever come my way."[21]

Ultimately, Bonhoeffer learned much more than he taught in New York. This was due largely to his involvement in Harlem, where for over six months he was a regular visitor. Bonhoeffer's love affair with the cultural Mecca of Negro America began with an invitation from fellow student Albert F. ("Frank") Fisher to visit Abyssinian Baptist Church. Captivated by the emotional style of worship and the powerful sermons of legendary preacher Adam Clayton Powell Sr., Dietrich became active in the church's ministry. He taught Sunday school, conducted a Bible study for Negro women, assisted in weekday church school, and visited in parishioners' homes. Bonhoeffer's connection with Harlem was enhanced in Reinhold Niebuhr's course "Ethical Viewpoints in Modern Literature"

and strengthened through reading black literature and listening to recordings of Negro spirituals.

Thus in less than a year Bonhoeffer experienced more of "Negro" culture than most American whites did in a lifetime. With Fisher he suffered the indignity of being refused service in a New York restaurant and felt the vicarious pride of visiting Howard University in Washington, D.C. Traveling by train through the South during the Christmas holidays, he witnessed segregation firsthand. He judged American apartheid to be a contradiction of the nation's ideals and commented that "the way the southerners talk about the Negroes is simply repugnant."[22]

In addition to Frank Fisher, three New York friends—Paul Lehmann, Erwin Sutz, and Jean Lasserre—had a lasting impact on Bonhoeffer. Sutz, the Swiss national with whom he traveled to Cuba at Christmastime, would introduce Dietrich to Karl Barth in the summer of 1931. Lasserre, the French pacifist who became his companion on a cross-country drive to Mexico, challenged Bonhoeffer with a perspective on the Sermon on the Mount that made Jesus' peace commandment inescapable. Lehmann was a tutor in systematic theology at Union who understood Bonhoeffer better than any American he encountered and, with his wife Marion, formed a surrogate family for the foreign student.

Bonhoeffer seized his American opportunity by exploring the country's culture and becoming acquainted with its "social gospel." Exposure to what was "remote from his previous experience" (as Lehmann put it) would pay long-term dividends. If at first he suspected that the political questions which captured the attention of American theology students were "irrelevant to the life of a Christian,"[23] this attitude would soon be challenged by events at home.

ANAN

## Liberation: Part Two

"In his personal life," Bethge writes of Bonhoeffer after his return from New York, "something occurred during these months that is hard for us to perceive fully, though its effects are plain. He himself would never have called it a conversion. But a change occurred in him."[24] Bonhoeffer himself later described this change as a turn from "the phraseological to the real." Its manifestations were quite visible to those who knew him: more regular church attendance, scriptural meditation, prayer, oral confession, and a pacifist interpretation of the Sermon on the Mount. There is only one surviving letter in which Dietrich discussed this spiritual development. In 1936 he wrote that he had

> plunged into work in a very unchristian way. An . . . ambition that many noticed in me made my life difficult.

23

Then something happened, something that has changed and transformed my life to the present day. For the first time I discovered the Bible. . . . I had often preached, I had seen a great deal of the church, spoken and preached about it—but I had not yet become a Christian.

I know that at that time I turned the doctrine of Jesus Christ into something of personal advantage for myself. . . . I pray to God that will never happen again. Also I had never prayed, or prayed only very little. For all my loneliness, I was quite pleased with myself. Then the Bible, and in particular the Sermon on the Mount, freed me from that. Since then everything has changed. I have felt this plainly, and so have other people about me. It was a great liberation.[25]

Both the timing of this "great liberation" and its exact nature are elusive. Bethge traces the change to 1931–1932 and links it to Bonhoeffer's dilemma regarding whether a theologian could also be a Christian. Clifford Green locates it in the summer of 1932 and believes it represents the outcome of Bonhoeffer's struggle with the ego that seeks to dominate others, a battle with personal ambition he had waged since 1927 and that is analyzed in his dissertations.[26] What we know for certain is that this "great liberation" left a lasting imprint on Bonhoeffer's thought and behavior and prepared him for the challenges that lay before him.

## And Berlin Again

Bethge identifies Bonhoeffer's return to Berlin in 1931 as the start of a second phase in his career. His period of "learning and roaming" at an end,[27] Bonhoeffer now began to labor diligently in three fields—the academic,

where he gave lectures and seminars at the university; the pastoral, in which he worked as a student chaplain; and the ecumenical, a new sphere of activity for the twenty-five-year-old.

As Bonhoeffer began to deliver lectures in a crowded department of systematic theology where many leaned toward National Socialism, a circle of faithful students gathered round. Noticing that something about the young teacher "intrinsically distinguished him from the behavior and ideals of a professor,"[28] students were meeting him for evening discussions in the city and weekend getaways at his cottage. In his lecture courses Bonhoeffer treated theological issues that had contemporary relevance, such as the "orders of creation" theology on which nationalists were relying to link Nazism with God's will. Although Bonhoeffer's career at Berlin lasted only four semesters, two of his lecture courses were published. *Creation and Fall: A Theological Exposition of Genesis 1–3* appeared at the time, and *Christ the Center,* based on student notes from his gripping 1933 lectures on Christology, was published posthumously.

Just as his academic career got under way, Bonhoeffer was ordained to the ministry of the church. This meant a practicum year, during which he would serve as chaplain and counselor to students at the technical college in Charlottenburg (later the Technical University of Berlin). His church superiors had high hopes for this new position, but Bonhoeffer's ministry at the technical college may charitably be called unfruitful. After two frustrating years of labor yielded a "quite modest" response among students, no successor was named.

Bonhoeffer enjoyed considerably more success with a confirmation class in the working class Zionskirche parish of eastern Berlin, which he called "just about the wildest district"[29] in the city. He inherited an unruly group of boys but won them over with stories of Harlem, invitations to an apartment he rented in the neighborhood, and trips to his weekend cottage outside the city. Bonhoeffer's attachment to these boys and his sensitivity to their needs led in the summer of 1932 to the creation of a "youth club," which flourished until Hitler came to power early the following year. Meanwhile Bonhoeffer tried to secure a full-time pastoral position at the Friedrichshain church in proletarian eastern Berlin, but the congregation found his preaching "too grand," and he was not appointed.

## Ecumenical Work

One aspect of Bonhoeffer's life that has received increased attention in recent years is his commitment to the burgeoning European ecumenical movement. Bonhoeffer expressed little interest in ecumenism before 1931, when he was made part of the German youth delegation to the annual conference of the World Alliance for Promoting

International Friendship through the Churches (a predecessor of the World Council of Churches). At the conference in Cambridge, England, Bonhoeffer was appointed honorary international youth secretary in the Alliance, thus becoming part of the organization's inner circle.

In 1931 a number of Berlin church leaders were prominent in international church work. But the ship of German ecumenism was increasingly beset by the winds of *völkisch* nationalism and eventually foundered on what was perceived as anti-German sentiment abroad. In the wake of growing anti-internationalism within Germany, Bonhoeffer became committed to the ecumenical cause. He spoke out against theologies that cast nation or *Volk* as direct reflections of God's will and developed a driving concern for international peace. An experimental catechism on which he collaborated with Franz Hildebrandt proclaimed that "the church knows nothing of any sacredness of war." In a lecture titled "Christ and Peace" he opined that "any form of war service, any preparation for war, is forbidden for the Christian." Obviously, Bonhoeffer's thinking on

the subject had changed dramatically since 1929, when he wrote that "love for my people will sanctify murder, will sanctify war."[30]

Bonhoeffer was something of a gadfly within the ecumenical movement, constantly reminding his fellow ecumenists of the need to clarify the theological basis for its existence. Is the World Alliance "the church," or simply an organization of well-meaning Christians, he asked insistently. If the church, then what concrete commandment does it have for the world? Bonhoeffer's own view was clear: "We are not an organization to expedite church action, but we are a definite form of the church itself."[31] The calls for international friendship that typically resulted from meetings of the World Alliance and other groups were welcome, of course, but Bonhoeffer believed these pronouncements distracted the ecumenical community from the theological and confessional tasks that should form the basis of its work. As he gained influence in ecumenical circles, Bonhoeffer's emphasis on these tasks gained a hearing.

After the Nazi revolution in Germany, Bonhoeffer's ecumenical work took on a new dimension—publishing abroad the true nature of Nazism and securing the international community's support in combating heresy within the German church. In September 1933 he attended the World Alliance conference in Sofia, Bulgaria, where he informed the organization's leadership about the anti-Jewish campaign in his country. The result was a resolution that decried "state measures against the Jews in Germany" and protested the church's exclusion of "non-Aryans" as "a denial of the explicit teaching and spirit of the Gospel of Jesus Christ."[32] Thus Bonhoeffer was able to make the German church struggle an international Christian concern.

## Struggle for the Church

In a letter to his brother Dietrich in 1931, Klaus Bonhoeffer lamented that Germans were "flirting with fascism." Within eighteen months the flirtation would become a fatal embrace. As the Nazi revolution unfolded, it became evident to Bonhoeffer that "academic discussion must give way to action."[33] For him it did so on February 1, 1933, just two days after Hitler's appointment as chancellor of the German Republic. In a radio address titled "The Younger Generation's Altered View of the Concept of *Führer*," Bonhoeffer warned that if a leader surrenders to the wishes of his followers, "then the image of the Leader [*Führer*] will gradually become the image of the misleader [*Verführer*]."[34] Although his microphone was mysteriously switched off before Bonhoeffer could utter this climactic warning, the address is unmistakable evidence of the clarity with which Bonhoeffer viewed the Nazi threat.

In the aftermath of a suspicious *Reichstag* fire later that month, Hitler acted to consolidate power through a series of acts and emergency decrees. Among these was the Law for the Restoration of the Professional Civil Service, which included a provision stipulating that "non-Aryans" (later defined to include anyone with three or four Jewish grandparents) could be summarily dismissed from civil service positions. As a symbol of their desire to align the German Evangelical Church with National Socialism, members of the Faith Movement of the German Christians campaigned to apply this "Aryan paragraph" in the ecclesiastical realm, thereby excluding pastors of Jewish background.

In mid-April, in an essay titled "The Church and the Jewish Question," Bonhoeffer addressed the issue of the "Aryan paragraph" and the church. Applying the Lutheran understanding of church-state relations to the new political situation, Bonhoeffer claimed that since the state is a divine order of preservation in a godless world, the church has no right to address it in its "history making actions." However, he added, the church *may* ask the state whether its actions are in conformity with its divine calling—whether, that is, they lead to law and order. "Both too much law and order and too little law and order compel the church to speak." Bonhoeffer concluded that there are three possible ways in which the church can act toward the state when it fails to exercise its divine vocation:

> In the first place, as has been said, it can ask the state whether its actions are legitimate and in accordance with its character as state, i.e., it can throw the state back on its responsibilities. Secondly, it can aid the victims of state action. The church has an unconditional obligation to the victims of any ordering of society, even if they do not belong in the Christian community. . . . The third possibility is not just to

bandage the victims under the wheel, but to put a spoke in the wheel itself [literally, "to fall into the spokes of the wheels"].[35]

In addition to an unusually clear articulation of the conditions for church resistance, what distinguishes this essay from other treatments of the "Jewish Question" at this time is Bonhoeffer's expression of concern for the fate of German Jews per se, whether or not they happened to be members of the Christian community.

In opposing German Christian attempts to bring the church into alignment with Nazi values, Bonhoeffer affiliated with a series of opposition groups active in the "church struggle"—the Young Reformation movement, the Pastors' Emergency League, and the Confessing Church. Ultimately, though, he would conclude that none of these associations were insightful enough to recognize that application of the Aryan paragraph was not *adiaphoron* (a matter of indifference) but *status confessionis* (a matter of heresy), or to see through the illusion that nazifying the church would be a boon to evangelism. "The question really is Germanism or Christianity," Bonhoeffer wrote in August 1933 with characteristic clarity.[36]

At a June meeting in Berlin, Bonhoeffer debated representatives of the German Christian movement before two thousand auditors. His argument centered on Romans 14, where Paul discusses those he calls "strong" and "weak" in faith. Some of Bonhoeffer's comrades in the church struggle, including Martin Niemöller, were invoking the Pauline typology to claim that non-Aryan pastors and officials should voluntarily remove themselves from the church out of respect for "weak" church members who could not tolerate their presence. Bonhoeffer pointed out, however, that while the "strong" may have to *bear* those who in their "weakness" must rely on law (i.e., the "Aryan paragraph"), the church must realize that a *triumph* of the weak may infect the body of Christ with heresy and bring schism.

In the run-up to church elections in July, Bonhoeffer protested at Gestapo headquarters that campaign pamphlets of the Young Reformation party had been illegally confiscated. Though his complaint was met with the prospect of being sent to a concentration camp, Bonhoeffer was undeterred. In September he was in Wittenberg nailing the manifesto "To the National Synod" to trees while delegates considered how far the church should go in enforcing racial conformity. In August Bonhoeffer was sent to Bethel as part of a working group charged with drafting a confession that would detail the theological convictions of the church opposition.

The Bethel Confession affirmed that God elected the Jews and continues to show "his faithfulness by still

keeping faith with Israel after the flesh," claimed that the barrier between Jew and Gentile is removed by the cruci-fixion and resurrection of Jesus Christ, endorsed Jewish evangelism, and opposed segregation in Jewish Christian communities. The confessors even asserted that "it is the task of Christians who come from the Gentile world to expose themselves to persecution rather than to surrender, willingly or unwillingly, even in one single respect, their brotherhood with Jewish Christians in the church, founded on Word and Sacrament."[37] But as the confession Bon-hoeffer had worked on passed through stages of the edito-rial process, its message of solidarity with Jews was so weakened that he refused to sign the final draft.

## London

"I have always wanted to be a pastor," Bonhoeffer wrote to Karl Barth in the fall of 1933, but fulfilling his dream of ministering in the German Evangelical Church would take him overseas again. Bonhoeffer had decided that he could not serve a church in which the pastoral calling had become a racial privilege. So when a position became available he was compelled to withdraw out of solidarity with his close friend, non-Aryan pastor Franz Hildebrandt. Hildebrandt later wrote that he could not "recall or imagine" anyone else taking this line of solidarity with the excluded pastors.[38]

When the Aryan paragraph was officially adopted in September at the general synod of the Evangelical Church of the Old Prussian Union (referred to as the "brown synod" because many delegates donned brown SA uniforms), Bonhoeffer began seriously to question whether he could remain in the German Evangelical Church at all. This concern, and frustration with his colleagues' willingness to compromise with the German Christian heresy, led him to accept a church position in London. "I found myself in radical opposition to all my friends[,] . . . increasingly isolated with my views of the matter," he wrote to Barth after arriving in England. "It was time," he had concluded, "to go into the wilderness for a spell."[39]

Given Bonhoeffer's prominent role in the church opposition, Theodor Heckel of the Church Foreign Office sought a guarantee of loyalty before approving this English assignment. But Bonhoeffer was adamant that he would not represent abroad a church dominated by German Christians. He was convinced, in fact, that adoption of the "Aryan paragraph" had effectively separated the Evangelical Church in Prussia from the Christian church, and his loyalties would always be to the latter. Against Heckel's better judgment Bonhoeffer was allowed to assume pastoral duties in London in the German congregations at Forest Hill and Sydenham. In addition to preaching and caring for souls in these parishes (which he encouraged to develop programs that would engage their children and youth),

Bonhoeffer sought to aid "countless German visitors, most of them Jews."

Bonhoeffer's most important role during this period was as de facto leader of the German pastors in England, a group he soon convinced to join the Pastor's Emergency League (an organization supporting Jewish-Christian pastors that grew out of a document of protest written by Bonhoeffer and Niemöller in September). Under Bonhoeffer's guidance, the pastors sent a series of telegrams to authorities in Berlin protesting steps taken by the church government under *Reichsbischopf* (Reich bishop) Ludwig Müller. These steps included the merging of the Evangelical Youth with the Hitler Youth and the "muzzling decree" of January 1934, which made it illegal to discuss or write about the church struggle. Urging resistance against the Berlin leadership, the émigré pastors leveraged the threat of withdrawal from the German Evangelical Church.

In order to pacify these refractory foreign clergymen and curtail their contact with the press and ecumenical groups, Heckel was compelled to visit London in February 1934. When he reminded them that "opposing [*Reichsbischopf*] Müller is tantamount to opposing the state," Bonhoeffer responded that secession was "the most urgent church policy task for today."[40] Heckel attempted unsuccessfully to extract a declaration of loyalty from the pastors, whom, he charged, had begun to submit to foreign influence. He also called Bonhoeffer to Berlin, where he instructed him to refrain from all ecumenical activity and made ominous remarks concerning his personal safety. But Bonhoeffer subtly resisted Heckel's demands and remained vague regarding his ecumenical commitments. Ironically, by summoning Bonhoeffer to Germany, Heckel allowed him to participate in the church opposition's first "free synod," where the national "Confessing synod" at Barmen was planned.

Due in part to his role as a primary signatory to the manifesto "To the National Synod," which had appeared in the British press, prominent Britons looked to Bonhoeffer as a reliable interpreter of the church-political situation in Germany. Through their common concern for the German church, Bonhoeffer became particularly close to George K. A. Bell, bishop of Chichester and chairman of the Universal Christian Council for Life and Work. Bonhoeffer sought to convince Bell and other ecumenical leaders that the movement needed to decide whether the Nazi-dominated Reich church or its opposition represented the genuine Evangelical Church in Germany. If it was not willing to make this judgment, Bonhoeffer wrote to Henry Louis Henriod, director of the World Alliance, "then the ecumenical movement is no longer church, but a useless association for making fine speeches."[41]

Bonhoeffer played a unique role in the German church struggle, for he was both leader and maverick. In London he guided his pastoral colleagues in defying the German church hierarchy, declaring that they belonged "inwardly" to the Confessing Church, proclaiming that the Aryan paragraph "contradicts the clear meaning of the scriptures,"[42] and initiating a mass secession of the English congregations from the Reich church. He also influenced a 1934 pastoral letter by Bishop Bell that decried the abuses of state and church in Germany.

But Bonhoeffer's call for separation from what he regarded as an apostate church was out of step with his colleagues in Germany. Even a close collaborator like Martin Niemöller seemed from Bonhoeffer's vantage point overly cautious. "Now is the time when we must be radical on all points, including the *Aryan paragraph*, without fear of the possible disagreeable consequences for ourselves," Bonhoeffer wrote to Niemöller in late 1933.[43] Before just about any other German Protestant, Bonhoeffer perceived the situation with stark clarity: "We are immediately faced with the decision: National Socialist *or* Christian."[44]

Bonhoeffer was not present at the Dahlem Confessing Synod (October 1934), which established emergency church administrations and called congregations to ignore the Reich church government and "adhere to the directions of the Confessional synod of the German Evangelical Church and its recognized bodies."[45] Yet Bonhoeffer took these synodal decisions more seriously than many of the confessors in Germany. Indeed, they were "beacons" that illuminated his path between 1934 and 1939, a path perceived as fanatical by those unwilling to risk being perceived as disloyal to the state.

In August 1934 Bonhoeffer participated in the biennial conference of the Universal Christian Council for Life and Work at Fanö, Denmark, where he was charged with organizing both a youth conference jointly sponsored by Life and Work and the World Alliance and a plenary lecture on the church and the world of nations. While preparing for these tasks, Bonhoeffer was concerned that the conference recognize the Confessing Church recently born at Barmen. Since the Church Foreign Office (led by Bonhoeffer's nemesis Heckel) had already been invited as the official representative of the German Evangelical Church, Bonhoeffer himself represented the Confessing Church at Fanö, where he was elected a member of the Universal Christian Council for Life and Work.

Bonhoeffer's plenary lecture, "The Universal Church and the World of Nations," was a source of considerable controversy, focused as it was not on practical questions but on the Christian obligation to maintain peace. His homily at morning worship the same day, in which he came as close as he ever would to pure pacifism, is "the most

unequivocal and emphatic of his statements on peace that we possess."[46] Bonhoeffer asked:

> How does peace come about? Through a system of political treaties? Through the investment of international capital in different countries? Through big banks, through money? Or through universal peaceful rearmament in order to guarantee peace? Through none of these, for the single reason that in all of them peace is confused with safety. There is no way to peace along the way of safety. For peace must be dared. It is the great venture. It can never be safe. Peace is the opposite of security.[47]

Not surprisingly, the Fanö Youth Conference also bore the imprint of Bonhoeffer's concerns with the church's transnational character and the ecumenical responsibility for peace. A casual beach conversation illumined one implication of Bonhoeffer's embrace of the peace commandment.

When asked what he would do in the event war broke out, Dietrich replied that he would pray for "the strength not to take up arms."[48]

Shortly after arriving in London, Bonhoeffer began to seriously consider a study trip to India. The plan seems to have had its genesis during Bonhoeffer's year in Barcelona, when his grandmother Julie Tafel Bonhoeffer suggested that he experience "the world of the East" and sent funds to encourage the adventure. He spoke of such a trip again in 1930 before departing for America; his plan was to return to Germany via Asia. In 1934 the scheme occupied Bonhoeffer's thoughts for a third time. He wrote to his grandmother that India had "more Christianity . . . than in the whole of our Reich Church,"[49] by which he meant that Gandhi exemplified Jesus' Sermon on the Mount better than Western Christians. Bonhoeffer was particularly intrigued by the possibility of applying nonviolent methods in resisting Nazi tyranny.

In England Bonhoeffer sought out Gandhi sympathizers and had his fitness for life in the tropics tested. A letter of introduction from George Bell informed Gandhi that his young German friend would be in India during early 1935 to "study community life as well as methods of training." Gandhi responded by inviting Bonhoeffer and a friend to "share my daily life . . . if I am out of prison."[50] But Dietrich remained torn between remaining in England, returning to the university, traveling to India, and starting a Protestant monastic community. In the end he would be drawn to the latter option under the aegis of the Confessing Church.

## Finkenwalde

In January 1935 Bonhoeffer shared with his brother Karl-Friedrich his belief that "the restoration of the church must surely depend on a new kind of monasticism, which has nothing in common with the old but a life of uncompromising discipleship, following Christ according to the Sermon on the Mount. I believe the time has come to gather people together and do this."[51]

The time had come, indeed. After Reich Bishop Müller closed the preachers' seminaries of the Old Prussian Union, the regional Council of Brethren (the emergency church administration of the Confessing Church) moved to provide for the training of its candidates apart from the universities. Bonhoeffer was offered the directorship of the new Confessing Church seminary in Berlin-Brandenburg, which was to open in early 1935. Before leaving England, he prepared for this assignment by visiting several Anglican religious communities, as well as colleges for the training of Methodist and Quaker candidates. At the end of April he met twenty-three would-be German preachers at

41

Zingst on the Baltic Sea; in mid-June they moved to a vacant building in the Pomeranian country town of Finkenwalde.

After several years of reflection on Christian communal life, Bonhoeffer now had the opportunity to build and oversee such a community. For two-and-a-half years he devoted himself to intense preparation of the men who would be faced with preserving the church against Nazi harassment and ecclesiastical indifference. Local Confessing Church congregations supported the seminary by contributing everything from furniture and musical instruments to live animals. Bonhoeffer donated his personal library and a remarkable collection of records that included American blues and spirituals. The seminary was also sustained by resident members of the landed aristocracy. One of Bonhoeffer's most ardent supporters was Ruth von Kleist-Retzow, grandmother of the young woman who would later become his fiancée.

The daily routine at Finkenwalde was scripted and intense. After sleeping together in one room, the candidates began their day around the dinner table with a forty-five-minute worship service that included hymn singing, Bible reading, and prayer. Before undertaking the day's theological work, students were to engage in half an hour of private meditation, their only guidance coming from the common scriptural text assigned for that week. It soon became clear that some of the ordinands were simply unprepared for this level of spiritual discipline. The unpopularity of the Finkenwalde routine came to light during a community discussion at which some complained about the length of prayers and lessons and others confessed to sleeping or working during "meditation." As a result, the schedule was adjusted to accommodate "group meditation" once or twice a week. Personal confession in preparation for the Eucharist was another communal practice with

which the ordinands were at first uncomfortable. But with Bonhoeffer modeling the attitudes and practices he sought to instill, discomfort and resistance eventually gave way to acceptance.

While life at Finkenwalde was governed by rules, time was set aside for bathing, table tennis, and music (there were two grand pianos), as well as free discussion of current issues; not surprisingly, these included the state's claims to loyalty and military service from individual Germans. A former student recalled that while Bonhoeffer did not insist that they refuse the call to military service, he made certain they would enlist with a troubled conscience. These men were being prepared for the inevitable. Nearly all of Bonhoeffer's 150 Finkenwalde students were conscripted, and more than 80 were killed in action during World War II.

The syllabus at Finkenwalde resembled that of other preachers' seminaries. It featured the teaching of homiletics (which included Bonhoeffer's evaluative strolls with the sermon's author), lectures on the ministry and the church, and study of Protestant confessional writings. Bonhoeffer's main curricular innovation—the series of lectures on discipleship that led in 1937 to the publication of *Nachfolge* (original English title, *The Cost of Discipleship*)—would become a distinctive feature of Finkenwalde. The book's best-known passage is the opening description of "cheap grace," but its theological crux is the statement that "only the believer is obedient and only those who are obedient believe." With this formulation Bonhoeffer forced together belief in Christ and Christ's authoritative demand for obedience in a way that was uncharacteristic of Lutheran theology.

After a few months at Finkenwalde Bonhoeffer developed a proposal designed to bring to life his dream of a more permanent, quasi-monastic community. The *Brü-dergemeinde*, or "house of brethren," was to consist of ordinands who would remain at Finkenwalde after completing their training and engage in a "concrete experiment in communal living and communal awareness of Christ's commandments."[52] The six candidates who received permission to join the "house of brethren" at Finkenwalde followed the seminary routine and pledged themselves to answer emergency calls from the church. This experiment in communal life was the basis for Bonhoeffer's book *Life Together* (1939), the text from his pen most widely read during his lifetime.

Despite the remoteness of Finkenwalde, the seminarians kept informed of church-political developments and were actively engaged in the Pomeranian church struggle. In September 1935, after hearing of a proposal that would implicitly endorse the recently enacted Nuremberg Laws revoking the citizenship of "non-Aryans," the Finken-waldeans attended the Old Prussian Confessing Synod at Steglitz to lobby against the resolution. After Bonhoeffer briefly resumed his university lectures in Berlin in late 1935, he was able to keep the seminarians' community aware of national developments.

As it turned out, information was traveling in both directions. Finkenwalde's unusual combination of intense study, practical piety, liturgical discipline, and communal living attracted attention in national and international church circles, not all of it positive. Suspicion hung over the seminary in part because of the activities and statements of its director. In early 1936 Bonhoeffer organized a group visit to Sweden without the approval of church officials in Berlin. This resulted in his termination as a university lecturer and a letter of warning calling him "a pacifist and an enemy of the state."[53] In April Bonhoeffer published a Bible study on Ezra and Nehemiah, whose rejection of their adversaries' offer to assist in rebuilding the temple, he pointed out, contained a lesson about the German church's relationship to the state. The study brought charges from the academic realm that Bonhoeffer had misused the Old Testament.

Bonhoeffer ignited a firestorm in June 1936 with an article claiming that "whoever knowingly separates himself from the Confessing church in Germany separates himself from salvation."[54] As we have seen, Bonhoeffer had long insisted that the international ecumenical movement could not evade the question whether the Reich Church or the Confessing Church represented the genuine body of

Christ. But his assertion that salvation hung on the answer brought Bonhoeffer new notoriety. In addition to being called a "fanatic" and "too Reformed," Bonhoeffer was now accused of "false doctrine," "legalism," and even "Romanism."

While Bonhoeffer continued to find support in ecumenical circles, he was continually frustrated by the movement's desire to maintain friendly contact with all church "parties" in Germany. He refused to attend several meetings in protest against participation by Reich Church representatives. Increasingly, those representatives expressed similar sentiments about Confessing Church delegations, placing the ecumenical leaders in a very difficult dilemma. In April 1937 Bonhoeffer's thorny relationship with Henriod was strained to the breaking point over the matter of representation at the Conference of World Churches at Oxford.

## Collective Pastorates

It was more than Bonhoeffer's demands and controversial claims that drew attention in his direction. From the perspective of the Reich Church leadership, the work he was doing at Finkenwalde had been illegal from the beginning, a view made official in December 1935 by a decree of the Reich Ministry for Church Affairs. "Everything we do here is now illegal and contrary to the law of the state,"[55] Bonhoeffer wrote at the time. Yet the work continued with only a few defections, even in 1937 when new regulations made it illegal to read from the pulpit the names of those who had left the church, to take up collections during Confessing Church services, or to circulate newsletters.

For the time being the state would not apply force directly against the Confessing Church, but many opposition churchmen became targets of persecution. When a wave of arrests in 1937 resulted in the imprisonment of over eight hundred confessors, Bonhoeffer made Finkenwalde a place of intercession, aid, and recuperation for the persecuted. But the seminary did not await the arrival of the needy. In mission tours throughout the region the Finkenwaldeans "evangelized" in small congregations that were standing firm against the encroachment of Nazism. At a time when the Reich bishop was intent on "Germanizing" the Sermon on the Mount, Bonhoeffer, his students, and his colleagues were dedicated to living it out.

In July 1937 Martin Niemöller was arrested and the offices of the Confessing Church's Provisional Administration sealed. Bonhoeffer himself had a run-in with the Gestapo when they returned to search Niemöller's parsonage and interrupted a meeting of Confessing Church leaders. Finkenwalde was finally shut down on September 28,

1937, the order to "dissolve" the seminary noting that "the long-standing practice of using their own organizations to train and examine young theologians in defiance of the institution set up by the state . . . is likely to endanger the state's authority and welfare."[56]

Bonhoeffer's response to the state's closing of Finkenwalde was to establish "collective pastorates" in which illegal candidates were apprenticed to Confessing Church clergymen in legal ministries. Between 1938 and 1940 (when conscription took most of them into the military) Bonhoeffer's ordinands worked as "apprentice vicars" in two remote parishes in eastern Pomerania. One group of up to ten candidates occupied the pastor's vicarage in Köslin, while another lived together forty miles away in the parsonage at Gross-Schlönwitz (this group relocated to Sigurdshof in early 1939). Bonhoeffer was registered as an assistant minister in the town of Schlawe, from which he traveled between the training sites twice each week.

Two church-political issues dominated Bonhoeffer's days with the collective pastorates. One was the loyalty oath all pastors in active office were ordered to take on Hitler's birthday (April 20) in 1938. The oath required that members of the clergy swear to "be faithful and obedient to Adolf Hitler, the *Führer* of the German Reich and people, [and] . . . conscientiously observe the laws and carry out the duties of my office, so help me God." With no official status in the church, Bonhoeffer was personally exempt from the vow; his concern was that the Confessing Church support pastors in resisting the decree. When the Confessing synod of the Old Prussian Union permitted its members to take the oath under certain cònditions, Bonhoeffer accused the body of causing "a rupture within its ranks."[57] In many provinces, between 60 and 90 percent of pastors were willing to affirm the oath, although many

"Dahlemites" (those who clung to the declarations of the Dahlem synod in which the confessors had set up a parallel church administration) resisted until the order was effectively overturned in August.

The second crisis of 1938 was brought about by an offer of legalization for pastors who had been trained, examined, and ordained by the Councils of Brethren under the provisions of the Dahlem synod. The young illegals could ensure they would be able to follow their pastoral calling by submitting to reexamination and acknowledging the authority of the church consistory. But Bonhoeffer could see legalization only as a decision to settle for "quietness and safety," helping oneself while abandoning one's brothers. He encouraged those under his influence to stand firm: "You may be suspended, removed, you may lose your income, be turned out of house and home, but you will again become preachers,"[58] Bonhoeffer wrote, quoting Zinzendorf.

As more and more men chose legalization, deep rifts in the church opposition became apparent. Addressing these divisions was difficult, because 1938 brought more travel restrictions, expulsion orders, and prohibitions against public speaking. Using these methods, the state limited communication between Confessing Church leaders without actually imprisoning them.

While the "Jewish Question" was not a central issue for the Confessing Church in 1938, it had become a grave concern for the Bonhoeffer family. Dietrich's twin sister Sabine and her "non-Aryan" husband, Gerhard Leibholz, were forced to emigrate in September. The fate of German Jews came to Bonhoeffer's attention again two months later when synagogues throughout the country were attacked and burned on *Kristallnacht*. After viewing some of the damage, Bonhoeffer opened his Bible and underlined in Psalm 74 the words "they burned all the meeting places of God in the land."

Many see in Bonhoeffer's response to the pogrom a turning point from church resistance to political conspiracy. Without doubt Bonhoeffer found the continued silence of the churches difficult to bear in the aftermath of *Kristallnacht*. "And the witnesses were silent" is how one scholar summarizes the Confessing Church's response to the "Jewish Question."[59] Bonhoeffer became increasingly discomforted by this silence and was determined to find a way to "speak out for the dumb" (Prov. 31:8).

## New York Again

After being required in late 1938 to record his place of residence in the "Military Registration Record," Bonhoeffer was ordered to report for a call-up on May 22, 1939. A one-year deferment secured through his father's

intervention temporarily mooted the question of conscientious objection. Still, Bonhoeffer began to seriously consider leaving Germany. When he traveled to England in March the possibility of emigration was foremost on Bonhoeffer's mind. As he explained in a letter to George Bell, his reasons for considering this possibility were opposition to the coming war and concern for his church:

> I am thinking of leaving Germany sometime. The main reason is the compulsory military service to which the men of my age will be called up this year. It seems to me conscientiously impossible to join in a war under the present circumstances. On the other hand the Confessional Church as such has not taken any definite attitude in this respect and probably cannot take it as things are. So I should cause a tremendous damage to my brethren if I would make a stand on this point which would be regarded by the regime as typical of our Church towards the State.[60]

As Larry Rasmussen has argued, this letter indicates that Bonhoeffer's conscientious objection to war service "under the present circumstances" arose not from a consistent pacifism but from a deep commitment to maintaining international peace.[61] The distinction is helpful for understanding how Bonhoeffer could within a year become involved in active resistance against the Third Reich.

During his five weeks in Britain, Bonhoeffer visited Bell, Willem Visser 't Hooft, the new general secretary of the provisional World Council of Churches (which was to succeed the existing ecumenical organizations), and Reinhold Niebuhr, who invited Bonhoeffer to visit their mutual friends in America. He was able to do so in June after an official teaching invitation from Union Theological Seminary won him a deferment from the army recruitment office. Having convinced the Confessing Church leadership that his presence in America could relieve the church's ecumenical isolation while keeping his attitude toward military service from becoming public, Dietrich left Germany on June 2 and sailed for the United States via England.

Upon his arrival in New York, Bonhoeffer learned that four separate American organizations had made plans for him. Despite this surfeit of opportunity, however, he almost immediately became "dreadfully homesick," his thoughts constantly turning to "the brothers" he had left behind in Pomerania. Following a restless evening wandering around Times Square, Bonhoeffer announced that he would be returning to Germany. He explained his decision in a letter to Niebuhr:

> I have made a mistake in coming to America. I must live through this difficult period of our national history with the Christian people of Germany. I will

have no right to participate in the reconstruction of Christian life in Germany after the war if I do not share the trials of this time with my people.[62]

Despite the protestations of Paul Lehmann and other American friends, on July 8 Bonhoeffer sailed home via England, deeply concerned with "the situation in Germany and in the church."

## Resistance

When Bonhoeffer arrived in Germany he went to eastern Pomerania and to the "brothers" whose training and well-being so concerned him. At the end of August the impending invasion of Poland forced him back to Berlin, but he later returned to Sigurdshof and remained with eight ordinands until the collective pastorates were dissolved in March 1940. Thereafter he spent a few months visiting congregations and pastors in East Prussia (in districts that are now part of Lithuania or Russia) as a Confessing Church "inspector."

Despite Bonhoeffer's low profile during this period, the state authorities remained aware of his activities. According to a secret report from July 1940, the Security Service (SD) knew that Bonhoeffer "only seldom resides at his domicile and appears there only in order to foster the impression that he has actually set up his residence in Pomerania. In fact, however, he travels continually through the entire country and holds Confessing Church gatherings in individual congregations."[63] As a result of his "activity subverting the people,"[64] Bonhoeffer was prohibited from speaking publicly anywhere in the Reich and was required to report his movements. A few months later his right to publish was rescinded "due to lack of the requisite political reliability."[65]

In a letter to the Reich Central Security Office (RHSA), Bonhoeffer forcefully rejected the charge of subversion, countering that "my entire outlook, my work as well as my background, make it inconceivable for me to allow myself to be identified with circles warranting the stigma of such a charge."[66] To emphasize that the regime had nothing to fear from him, Bonhoeffer concluded the letter with "Heil Hitler!" In truth, however, Bonhoeffer had already become allied with the anti-Nazi resistance through relatives in Berlin. He had been banned from the capital since January 1938, but through Karl Bonhoeffer's intervention gained permission to visit his parents' home. While technically confined there, he could justify the trips to Berlin through which he stayed abreast of developments in the resistance.

Plans for a coup d'état had been under discussion since 1938 when military and civilian leaders learned that Hitler intended to launch a new war. While the Führer's diplomatic and military successes made it difficult for the resistors to act at that point, hopes for an overthrow were renewed in late 1939 as stories of SS (*Schutzstaffel)* atrocities in Poland became known. Bonhoeffer's brother-in-law Hans von Dohnanyi incorporated reports and films of the Polish massacres into a record of Nazi crimes he had been collecting since 1933. This "chronicle of shame" was circulated among sympathetic generals who were resentful of SS and Gestapo encroachment on military authority, but the unexpected German victory over France in June 1940 again complicated plans for a putsch. When Hitler's so-called commissar order legalizing the immediate execution of Soviet political officers became known in 1941, the opposition appealed to the honor of German military commanders. However, the initial success of the Soviet invasion militated against a coup.

Bonhoeffer's chief contact with the resistors was Dohnanyi, his sister Christine's husband, who in 1939 had joined the *Abwehr* (Military Intelligence), an epicenter of anti-Hitler resistance headed by Admiral Wilhelm Canaris. The deputy Abwehr head was Colonel Hans Oster, who in 1940 warned the Dutch of Germany's impending attack. Bonhoeffer's association with the Abwehr commenced shortly after Dohnanyi joined Canaris's staff. His assignment in the intelligence service, Dohnanyi testified under interrogation in 1943, allowed Dietrich "to do his part for the armed forces" while capitalizing on his "international connections in the ecumenical sector."[67] In reality, being declared officially indispensable for work with Military Intelligence enabled Bonhoeffer to avoid conscription. His Abwehr assignments, furthermore, were undertaken on behalf of the conspirators.

Thus Bonhoeffer began the double life of a "confidential agent." With his military exemption and passport, he was able to move relatively freely during the war. Nevertheless, it was an unsettled and lonely existence. Many friends, particularly those abroad, concluded that he had switched sides in order to save his own skin. And although he could devote himself to working on the book that became *Ethics*, his theological work was now divorced from the communal experience of Finkenwalde and the collective pastorates. In fact, as Bonhoeffer's circular letters announcing the demise of former "brothers" indicate, his students were being decimated in Hitler's suicidal war. Family, of course, remained Bonhoeffer's lifeline. He spent a good deal of time at his parents' home in Berlin and boarded with his aunt in Munich after being assigned to the Abwehr office there.

After several weeks at the Benedictine monastery in Ettal, where he worked on *Ethics* and met inconspicuously

with resistance contacts, in February 1941 Bonhoeffer embarked on his first journey for Military Intelligence. He traveled to Switzerland, charged with resuming communication with associates in the Allied countries, confirming that the German resistance was still active, and utilizing these figures' influence in their own nations to ensure support for a post-putsch government. While there, Bonhoeffer explained to a curious Karl Barth why he was able to travel on a German passport issued by the SD. During a second visit to Switzerland in September 1941, Bonhoeffer passed along word of a coming revolt and requested that the Allies suspend military activity in the coup's aftermath.

Bonhoeffer journeyed to Norway in April 1942—officially to observe resistance in the Norwegian church as a possible danger to the German occupation, secretly to strengthen the anti-Nazi church opposition. In May he visited Switzerland a third time to notify the Allies that the German resistance was actively working to overthrow Hitler but needed established peace terms in order to win the cooperation of key generals. At the end of May he departed suddenly for neutral Sweden to meet Bishop Bell, through whom he would make contact with the British government and obtain safeguards for the coup. Bonhoeffer produced a list of the conspirators and revealed that the putsch would be initiated by two units at the front. He requested that, in the event of an overthrow, the Allies desist from belligerence until the new government could "restore healthy conditions" in Germany. Bonhoeffer and Bell agreed on coded methods of communication for further contacts between London and the resistance.

It had become clear to the conspirators that a change of government must begin with Hitler's assassination. Bonhoeffer reconciled himself to this decision and supported

it. Yet the longer the war continued without tangible signs of resistance within Germany, the more difficult became the task of obtaining guarantees from the enemy should Hitler be removed. The Allied governments tended increasingly to identify Germany with Nazism and thus were unlikely to enter peace negotiations with members of the military establishment. With his intimate knowledge of the "other Germany" represented by Bonhoeffer and his fellow resistors, Bishop Bell stressed to his contacts in the British government that "Germany and National Socialism are not the same thing."[68] But the distinction was becoming increasingly dim in the fog of war.

Bonhoeffer had great confidence in Bell. Yet despite his connections and his seat in the House of Lords, the bishop could not convince Foreign Secretary Anthony Eden to send the German resistance an encouraging reply through

Bonhoeffer. Bell stressed the Allies' interest in preparing for the new European order that would follow the defeat of Hitler. But his case, like Bonhoeffer's, was weakened by the absence of visible challenges to the Führer's power. In March 1943, as Bell sought to influence the British government to abandon its policy of unconditional surrender, a revolt was finally in the offing. Bonhoeffer and the other conspirators waited anxiously for news of an explosion aboard Hitler's airplane. Dohnanyi personally transported the explosive device in his briefcase, but once aboard the aircraft it failed to detonate. A new assassination plan called for a member of Military Intelligence to become a suicide bomber. As they awaited the outcome of this plot, Bonhoeffer, his brother Klaus, and brothers-in-law Dohnanyi and Rüdiger Schleicher (husband of Bonhoeffer's sister Ursula) were practicing a cantata for Karl Bonhoeffer's seventy-fifth birthday. The plot was foiled when Hitler cut short his tour of a military arsenal where the attack was to occur. Finally, there was the ill-fated plot of July 20, 1944, in which Claus Schenk Graf von Stauffenberg managed to smuggle a bomb into Hitler's lair, only to have the Führer survive the blast.

Bonhoeffer was aware of and in sympathy with all these plots, but this was not the extent of his subversive activity. He used his connections to obtain deferments for Confessing Church clergy who were targeted for military or labor conscription and sought to expose and undermine Nazi Jewish policy. In October 1941, for instance, Bonhoeffer gathered and compiled information on the deportation of Jews from Berlin. The resulting report was circulated among military leaders in the hope they would intervene or revolt outright and was sent to Geneva with the request that it be passed on to U.S. State Department officials and other diplomats. Bonhoeffer was also involved in a rescue

action known as "Operation 7," devised by Canaris and Dohnanyi to spirit fourteen Jews to neutral Switzerland on the pretext that they were Abwehr agents. Bonhoeffer supported the operation by calling on his Swiss contacts and was instrumental in getting Charlotte Friedenthal included in the group of rescuees.

## Arrest and Imprisonment

The drama of Bonhoeffer's anti-Nazi resistance was played out in a gray zone between rival secret services—the relatively independent Abwehr and Reinhard Heydrich's RHSA, which controlled the state police apparatus. Bonhoeffer was caught up in this rivalry in March 1941 when, despite his status as a "militarily indispensable" Abwehr worker, the Gestapo prohibited him from activity as a writer. Then, in the wake of the great troop losses at Stalingrad in March 1943, Bonhoeffer received a new order to report for military duty and was able to avoid conscription only with the protection of Canaris and Dohnanyi. While Canaris remained untouchable for the time being, Bonhoeffer, Dohnanyi, and Dohnanyi's wife, Christine (Bonhoeffer's sister), were arrested April 5, 1943, in a concerted effort by the RHSA to bring down the Military Intelligence Office.

Bonhoeffer was taken to Berlin-Tegel Military Detention Center and placed in the solitary confinement ward. He spent the next eighteen months in a seven-by-ten-foot cell with a wooden bed, a bench, a stool, and a bucket. The terrible homesickness he felt during his first sojourn in New York returned, and he briefly considered suicide. Eventually, though, Bonhoeffer rejected every form of self-pity and made the most of his time at Tegel with a daily routine that included physical exercise, meditation, Scripture memorization, and writing. One thing that brought him hope in prison was the promise of married life. On a visit to Klein-Krössin in 1942 he had become reacquainted

with Ruth von Kleist's granddaughter Maria von Wede-meyer, and they were engaged a few months later. After Bonhoeffer's arrest, Maria moved to Berlin to be near him, although her prison visits were always supervised. "We have been engaged for nearly a year," Bonhoeffer wrote, "and have never been alone together for one hour!"[69]

Among the documents that illuminate Bonhoeffer's state of mind while he languished in Tegel prison is a collection of letters between Dietrich and Maria written between July 1943 and December 1944. There are also letters to and from his parents from the period between April 1943 and January 1945 (at first Bonhoeffer was allowed a one-page letter every ten days, but the volume of correspondence increased when he found illegal delivery channels). Finally, there is the correspondence with Eberhard Bethge, most of which has been preserved in *Letters and Papers from Prison*. Together these documents provide an indispensable record of Bonhoeffer's experiences, emotions, and theological reflections during the Tegel period.

When Bonhoeffer's interrogation at the Reich War Court began a few days after his arrest, crucial issues for clarification were the date and circumstances of his Abwehr exemption. The interrogator charged, not incorrectly, that the Abwehr had assisted Bonhoeffer in evading military service, circumventing the Gestapo ban on public speaking, and continuing his church work. Bonhoeffer's initial strategy was to pose as a churchman completely inexperienced in military matters. But he had to avoid contradicting the testimony of other prisoners, particularly Dohnanyi. Family members helped ensure that their stories remained consistent by circulating books containing faint coded messages between the men's prisons.

During months of interrogation, Bonhoeffer portrayed

himself as a patriotic German in search of an effective channel for service to his fatherland. This portrait was drawn with claims that he had returned from the United States in 1939 to make himself available to the armed forces, that his Abwehr assignment provided "the war work" he had sought since the beginning of hostilities, and that putting his ecumenical connections to military use was a welcome opportunity to rehabilitate himself in the eyes of the state. As for the charge that he had subverted the war effort by avoiding conscription, Bonhoeffer responded that as a Christian he was not capable "of so serious a crime against the obvious duty of a German toward one's people and

Reich." These sensibilities were evident, he wrote to inter-rogator Manfred Roeder, in his choice of a future wife from a family of the German officer class, "all of whose fathers and sons have served in the field as officers since the beginning of the war, many serving with the highest decorations and making the ultimate blood sacrifice."[70]

Bonhoeffer also was forced to defend his efforts to secure Abwehr exemptions for Confessing Church pastors. He maintained that in recruiting colleagues for the intelligence service, he had done "everything possible to achieve the smoothest and greatest possible war effort on the part of the church."[71] Another serious charge facing Bonhoeffer was that Operation 7 was not an intelligence action but an attempt to sabotage Nazi Jewish policy. This accusation was successfully refuted with the help of Canaris, who was able to establish that the operation was planned prior to the deportation of German Jews. Nevertheless, the Reich War Court saw it as indicative of Bonhoeffer's "inner orientation" that he had tried to use his Abwehr connections to assist a non-Aryan held in a French transit camp.

Given this sustained effort to mislead his captors, it is not surprising that in prison Bonhoeffer was at work on an essay titled "What Does It Mean to Tell the Truth?" In it he reasoned that "depending on the person to whom I am speaking, the person who is questioning me, or what I am discussing, my word, if it seeks to be truthful, must vary."[72] Whether or not Bonhoeffer's subterfuge was justifiable, it was ultimately ineffective. In September Bonhoeffer was officially charged with subversion of the military forces, in part for "having undertaken . . . to evade . . . military service through measures based on deceit."[73] A trial was set for December, although the lawyers overseeing his case sought delays in the interest of the other imprisoned conspirators. In April 1944, still with no trial date in sight,

Bonhoeffer wrote, "I am really losing interest in my case. I often quite forget it for weeks on end."[74]

One useful distraction was the intellectual work Bonhoeffer was able to pursue. During his months in Tegel, he read voraciously on a variety of topics including early church history, contemporary science and philosophy, and nineteenth-century German literature. Soon after arriving at the prison he began writing a play and a novel, but it was his theological reflections in letters to Eberhard Bethge between April and August 1944 that were to have lasting significance. Bonhoeffer imagined the form faith would take in the ruins of the "Christian West" by invoking the concepts "world come of age," "religionless Christianity," and "arcane discipline," each of which continues to be discussed by theologians. The unfinished manuscript that explored these concepts has been lost; what remain are the so-called theological letters and an "Outline for a Book."

A remarkable aspect of Bonhoeffer's eighteen months in Tegel prison is the relationships he developed with prisoners and guards alike. He took walks with the prison commandant and played chess with his wardens; he was appointed medical orderly for his block and allowed to minister in sick bay; he was asked to write a report on improving the prison's air-raid procedures. Humane and sympathetic guards supplied Bonhoeffer with paper, smuggled his letters in and out, and sought assignment to his section so they could engage him in conversation.

It did not hurt that Bonhoeffer was related to General Paul von Hase, the city commandant of Berlin, who visited him in prison. But the respect he commanded in Tegel was based primarily on his peaceful demeanor and his willingness to minister to men in distress. A fellow prisoner wrote after the war that Bonhoeffer was "the best and the most gifted man I have ever met."[75] We know from Bonhoeffer's prison poem "Who Am I?" however, that the views of others did not always coincide with his self-perceptions:

> Who am I? They often tell me,
> I step out from my cell,
> Composed, contented and sure,
> Like a lord from his manor.
>
> Who am I? They often tell me,
> I speak with my jailers,
> Frankly, familiar and firm,
> As though I was in command.
>
> Who am I? They also tell me,
> I bear the days of hardship,
> Unconcerned, amused and proud,
> Like one who usually wins.
>
> Am I really what others tell me?
> Or am I only what I myself know of me?

Troubled, homesick, ill, like a bird in a cage,
Gasping for breath, as though one strangled me,
Hungering for colors, for flowers, for songs of birds,
Thirsting for kind words, for human company,
Quivering with anger at despotism and petty insults,
Anxiously waiting for great events,
Helplessly worrying about friends far away,
Empty and tired of praying, of thinking, of working,
Exhausted and ready to bid farewell to it all.

Who am I? This or the other?
Am I then, this today and the other tomorrow?
Am I both at the same time? In public, a hypocrite
And by myself, a contemptible, whining weakling?
Or am I to myself, like a beaten army,
Flying to disorder from a victory already won?

Who am I? Lonely questions mock me.
Who I really am, you know me, I am thine,
    O God![76]

After the failed assassination attempt of July 20, 1944, a guard named Knobloch offered to "disappear" with Bonhoeffer. Members of his family supplied money, food, and a mechanic's uniform Dietrich was to don as a disguise. But the plan was abandoned when the arrests of Klaus Bonhoeffer and Rüdiger Schleicher and the execution of Paul von Hase convinced Bonhoeffer that an escape would endanger family members.

Slowly Bonhoeffer came to terms with the likelihood that he would not survive the Nazi regime. "Stages on the Way to Freedom," a poem composed after the failed July 20 plot, concluded with a stanza titled "Death":

Come now, highest feast on the way to everlasting
    freedom,
Death. Lay waste the burdens of chains and walls
Which confine our earthly bodies and blinded souls,

That we see at last what here we could not see.
Freedom, we sought you long in discipline, action
  and suffering.
Dying, we recognize you now in the face of God.[77]

## Final Days

Bonhoeffer's arrest in April 1943 had deprived him of his freedom, and the failed July 20 plot had placed him under intensified scrutiny. His fate was sealed in late September 1944 with the discovery of a cache of secret documents stored in an underground safe in Zossen, a town southeast of Berlin that housed a series of military bunkers and was the headquarters for the Supreme Command of the Armed Forces. Although Dohnanyi's "chronicle of shame" had apparently been moved to a safer location, the hiding place in Zossen was betrayed and a number of incriminating documents discovered, including plans for a coup d'état, references to secret discussions with the British government via the Vatican, excerpts from the diary of Admiral Canaris, and correspondence related to Bonhoeffer's resistance activities. The Gestapo now had proof of an extensive conspiracy in the Abwehr.

Discovery of the Zossen files spelled the end for Dohnanyi, Oster, Canaris, and Bonhoeffer. His involvement in the Abwehr conspiracy confirmed, Bonhoeffer was transferred to the cellar of the RHSA prison on Prinz-Albrecht Strasse in central Berlin and confined in a five-by-eight-foot cell with a table, stool, and bed. Bonhoeffer

spent the next four months here, living on coffee, bread, and soup, bathing in unheated water, and enduring repeated Allied air raids. Although it is unlikely that he was subjected to torture, he found the repeated interrogations "frankly repulsive." The rigorous investigation that followed discovery of the Zossen files kept the five members of the Bonhoeffer family who were in Gestapo custody alive longer than some other conspirators, yet it all but ensured their ultimate demise. In February 1945 Klaus Bonhoeffer and Rüdiger Schleicher were the first to be sentenced to death.

We possess almost no record of Bonhoeffer's days following his transfer from Tegel. A significant exception is his best-known poem "By Kindly Powers Surrounded," which he wrote for Maria von Wedemeyer at the end of

1944 and which reveals an unshaken faith in God's goodness:

> By kindly powers surrounded, peaceful and true,
> Wonderfully protected with consolation dear,
> Safely, I dwell with you this whole day through,
> And surely into another year.[78]

Although he was deprived of regular visits from his parents and fiancée while at Prinz-Albrecht Strasse prison, Bonhoeffer did come into contact with some of the conspirators who were also prisoners of the Gestapo. These included Canaris, Dohnanyi, and Fabian von Schlabrendorff, Maria's cousin, who reported that when an Allied bombing raid on February 3 scored a direct hit on the basement of the RHSA, Bonhoeffer "remained quite calm, he did not move a muscle, but stood motionless and relaxed as if nothing had happened."[79] Four days later Bonhoeffer was among twenty prisoners loaded on trucks for transfer to concentration camps. He was transported in handcuffs to Buchenwald, where he and several others spent the next two months in air-raid shelter cells built beneath the houses of camp officials. Fellow prisoner Payne Best later shared his impressions of Dietrich during their Buchenwald sojourn:

> Bonhoeffer was all humility and sweetness; he always seemed to diffuse an atmosphere of happiness, of joy in every smallest event in life; and of deep gratitude for the mere fact that he was alive. . . . He was one of the very few men I have ever met to whom his God was real and ever close to him.[80]

On April 3, 1945, Bonhoeffer was evacuated from Buchenwald along with a truckload of "special prisoners." They traveled south, arriving in Schönberg on April 8, a

Sunday. Shortly after Bonhoeffer had led a worship service for the prisoners, two men appeared and demanded that he accompany them. According to Best, Bonhoeffer's last words were a message for Bishop Bell: "Tell him that for me this is the end but also the beginning—with him I believe in the principle of our Universal Christian brotherhood which rises above all national interests."[81]

In a meeting on April 5, Hitler had decided that Dohnanyi and Bonhoeffer were not to survive the Reich's demise. On April 7 a summary court-martial was being prepared for Bonhoeffer, Canaris, Oster, and others at Flossenbürg concentration camp. After interrogations that lasted late into the night, Bonhoeffer was hanged early the morning of April 9. Those who assisted in the executions of these enemies of the state received an extra ration of schnapps and blood sausage. Bonhoeffer's body was burned and his ashes mingled with those of other victims of the Third Reich.

A final glimpse of Bonhoeffer's life comes to us from the camp doctor at Flossenbürg:

> On the morning of that day between five and six o'clock the prisoners . . . were taken from their cells and the verdicts of the court martial read out to them. Through the half-open door in one room of the huts I saw Pastor Bonhoeffer, before taking off his prison garb, kneeling on the floor praying fervently to his God. I was most deeply moved by the way this unusually lovable man prayed, so devout and so certain that God heard his prayer. At the place of execution, he again said a short prayer and then

climbed the steps to the gallows, brave and composed. His death ensued after a few seconds. In the almost fifty years that I worked as a doctor, I have hardly ever seen a man die so entirely submissive to the will of God.[82]

# CHAPTER TWO

## Christ Existing as Community

First-time readers of Dietrich Bonhoeffer's theology are sometimes overwhelmed by the interrelatedness of each part of his work. A student in a recent semester-length seminar on Bonhoeffer exclaimed in frustration, "Every theme in Bonhoeffer is related to every other theme in Bonhoeffer! How am I supposed to choose a single research paper topic?" While this difficulty is real, it actually points to the continuity, beauty, and power of his thought.

This chapter begins to outline key theological themes in Bonhoeffer's corpus. Five themes tie the whole of Bonhoeffer's work together: (1) Christ existing as community,

(2) costly grace, (3) *Stellvertretung* ("vicarious representative action"), (4) ethics as formation, (5) and religionless Christianity. Each of these themes requires explanation; each is best understood in light of Bonhoeffer's steadfast reflection on the concept of suffering and profound commitment to the centrality of Christ; and each is addressed in turn in the pages and chapters that follow.

## Christ Existing as Community

It is not an overstatement to say that the central ideas of Bonhoeffer's theological work are present in or informed by his dissertation *Sanctorum Communio: A Dogmatic Inquiry into the Sociology of the Church.* Completed when he was twenty-one years old, the book considered the church as a reality in which "Christ exists as community." As the congregation gathers and experiences together God's grace in word, sacrament, and service, the church as community becomes the presence of Christ in the world. "Christ existing as community" is also a pivotal concept in both *Act and Being: Transcendental Philosophy and Ontology in Systematic Theology* (1929) and *Life Together* (1938). As Bonhoeffer continued to develop his understanding of this idea, he drew support from sociology, anthropology, ecclesiology (reflection on the church), Christology, and ethics.

In general, Bonhoeffer's concept of "Christ existing as community" has implications for being human, being in relation to other humans, the (ongoing) incarnation of Christ, and the structure and shape of the church (as community). But none of these ideas are expressed as simply as one might hope. *Sanctorum Communio* examines the sociological structure of the church and the theological place of Christ incarnate. Bonhoeffer is explicit in the

preface to this text that he will employ social philosophy and sociology in the service of theology. He claims that his investigation reveals the sociality of theology, that is, "the social intention of all the basic Christian concepts."[1] The implications of this claim are profound.

Among the most basic of Christian concerns is the nature of humanity: what does it mean to be human? For Bonhoeffer, the answer is clear. Human beings exist only in relationship to, and responsibility for, other human beings. This relationship comprises the social intention, or sociality, of theology. The Other (the You) makes an ethical claim on me and stands as a barrier or boundary to the self, to my I. When I encounter an Other, when the will of the

Other stands against my own will, I am called to respond, to answer. I am accountable. <u>For Bonhoeffer, the person *is* in encounter with and response to an Other.</u>

The Christian conception of the person offered by Bonhoeffer contains an important ethical dimension. "I and You are not interchangeable concepts, but comprise specific and distinct spheres of experience," he writes.[2] This distinction carries ethical import because it recognizes the Other *as* Other; it maintains the particularity and integrity of the Other. It also marks a break with the philosophical tradition, including its Kantian branch, in which Bonhoeffer was educated and in which the I was the starting point

for knowing (or not knowing, Bonhoeffer would argue) the self, the other, God, and the world.

In Immanuel Kant's famous critiques of reason, written at the end of the eighteenth century, he sought to analyze critical uses of reason and raise questions about how we *know* things. These are epistemological questions. Our knowledge, he claimed, requires a synthesis of our sense intuitions, or observations of a thing (the phenomenon), with the thing-in-itself (the noumenon), which is independent of the senses. Kant wondered what and how much the understanding and reason could know apart from experience. He concluded that nothing apart from a union of universality (the concept) and particularity (the sense experience) could be *known*. That which falls outside sense reality is *transcendent*. We can think about ideas of God and the soul, for example, but there are no sense perceptions that accompany these thoughts; we cannot *know* God.

Fundamental to Kant's project is the idea that human reason is limited. The thinking I is no longer at home—as was the case in precritical times—in the transcendent realm. Yet, perhaps ironically, the self stands alone as the starting point for reflection without reference to the conditions of history or presence of neighbor. This autonomous self is foundational to the enterprise known as *modernity*, or in Kant's terms, *transcendental philosophy*. In Kant's critiques of reason, the I (subject) always stands outside and apart from that which it thinks about (object); the mind functions as a mirror, seeking "truth" that it assumes is an accurate reflection of external reality. Postmodern critics of the Enlightenment reject the universality of the modern I and speak, instead, of the reflexive I, which is at least partially aware of its own social, historical, geographical, linguistic (and so on) location. The differences in these two worldviews, especially with regard to the relationship between I and You, are significant.

In the Kantian realm, the I experiences another person only as an Other I, reduced to a reflection of one's own (putatively universal) self and an object of one's thought. For Bonhoeffer, by contrast, the I-You relationship is not conceived as a subject-object relationship, where I am the subject and You are an object of my thinking. Rather, the You-form is by definition "the Other who places before me an ethical decision."[3] Bonhoeffer is not vague on this

point. The person, he claims, exists "always and only" in ethical responsibility.

For Bonhoeffer the coming to be of a person is tied to a moment, a moment of address or challenge, a moment of being moved or confronted. The creation of a person, he says, happens "in the situation of responsibility, passionate ethical struggle, confrontation by an overwhelming claim; thus the real person grows out of the concrete situation."[4] It is in this moment that one recognizes both the ethical boundary and the ethical demand represented by the Other. The I comes to be only in relation or response to the You; the You calls the I to responsible action and hence to ethical being. (Questions or claims about being are *onto-logical* questions and claims.)

Bonhoeffer's understanding of this relationship between I and You, also known as *intersubjectivity*, differs from the transcendental philosophy and ontology of Kant; in fact, it transforms the understanding of the cognitive self as the starting point for defining the Other, which is a hallmark of transcendental thinking. For Bonhoeffer the concept of the You as the "other I" is misleading. I cannot know the Other as an other I, only as a discrete and other You. In this way, Bonhoeffer prefigures postmodern thinkers in embracing an understanding of the relationship between I and Other based on dialogue; Bonhoeffer's intersubjectivity is a *dialogical* relationship.

For some readers, Bonhoeffer's understanding of the I-You relationship may seem reminiscent of the ideas in Martin Buber's well-known text *I and Thou* (1923). But Bonhoeffer did not know Buber's work, and while Bonhoeffer and Buber share some common ground, their fundamental approaches to the I-You relation diverge. Buber emphasizes an intimacy in the I-You relation that is absent in Bonhoeffer's thought. Like Buber, Bonhoeffer resists objectifying the Other, but Bonhoeffer conceives the Other as a boundary to the self and underscores the ethical encounter rather than intimacy between self and other. Some scholars worry that Bonhoeffer's understanding of the ethical encounter, even coupled with an emphasis on dialogue, is insufficient for sustaining relationships or establishing and sustaining community. But the concrete, communal practices Bonhoeffer used at the preachers' seminary in Finkenwalde not only embodied the theology of his early work but served to resolve this concern.

*Life Together*, which reflects the Finkenwalde experience, is replete with practical recommendations for living in community as the body of Christ, recommendations that create a sustained relation between each I and each Other

and that overcome the isolated encounters that fail to secure the continuity of life together. In *Life Together* Bonhoeffer advocates beginning each day at an early hour with a communal worship service of praise, hymn singing, psalm reading, and prayer. The day, he says, is to be spent alone in work and silence with only a brief respite for shared prayers of thanksgiving at midday. Solitude and community are mutually dependent. As the workday ends, the community is to gather once again to share a meal and a final service of worship. With singing, reading, and praying, the day ends as it began.

Overall, according to Bonhoeffer, community life should consist of time together, time alone, service, confession, and the Lord's Supper. These recommendations are not arbitrary rules; instead, each plays a vital role in creating and sustaining Christian community as Bonhoeffer envisioned (and lived) it. Each deepens our understanding of "Christ existing as community" and highlights the connections among *Sanctorum Communio, Act and Being,* and *Life Together.*

The relationship between I and You as described again and again by Bonhoeffer is not a direct relationship, but one mediated by the Divine You. One person cannot create, as it were, another person (by presenting that other with an ethical demand). Rather, when the You calls the I to ethical responsibility, it does so in unison with the Divine You. Human persons, each I and each You, are created by the Divine You. Consequently, one's real relationship with another person is a relationship mediated by God. This mediated relationship is, in essence, Bonhoeffer's theological anthropology. Implicit in this anthropology is the critical role of Bonhoeffer's understanding of the incarnation. In fact, it is not possible to talk about Bonhoeffer's conception of the person or his hopes for the revelatory "Christ existing as community" without also exploring his thoughts about Christ's presence in and action for the world.

Jesus Christ, Bonhoeffer asserts, appears to humanity as the self-revelation of God, the free disclosure of God's love. In Christ's suffering and dying for the whole of humanity, he acts vicariously and representatively on behalf of all. This vicarious act opens the possibility for those who follow after him—namely, Christians, to act accordingly. It is Christ's action that provides the model for life in community, and life in community that presents—to the world—the ever renewed incarnation of Christ. In Bonhoeffer's words:

> The "*sanctorum communio*" is the community based on Christ's vicarious representative action suffering on our behalf, and it consists of Christians on earth who in turn stand up for-each-other. The marks of the Church, if understood comprehensively, always imply the sociality of the church-community. The proclamation of the gospel and the celebration of the sacraments make Christ's vicarious representative action [*Stellvertretung*] present for us; and this vicarious representative action in turn finds expression in the church's social form.[5]

This vision of "Christ existing as community" is not eschatological (that is, concerned with what happens at the end of time); it is the formulation of Bonhoeffer's understanding of the visible community, both active and necessary, in the world in which we live. "Christian community," he writes in *Life Together*, "is not an ideal we have to realize, but rather a reality created by God in Christ in which we may participate."[6] The inseparability of the christological and ecclesiological in this statement is key, and the

foundation Bonhoeffer lays with regard to the Christian—
that is, social—concept of "person" paramount. "The
Christian person," writes Bonhoeffer, "achieves his or her
essential nature only when God does not encounter the
person as a You, but 'enters into' the person as I."[7]

And while persons come into ethical being in a particular place and time, the *essential* nature of humanity is not
tied to historical contingencies. Rather, essential human
nature is linked inextricably with the vicarious act—the
vicarious death—of Christ on behalf of humanity. As
scholar Clifford Green notes, "Bonhoeffer builds up his
argument to the position where humanity as a whole is the
'I' standing before God as the 'You.' Adam 'represents'
and 'personifies' created and fallen humanity before God;
Christ represents and personifies God before humanity and
the 'new humanity' before God."[8] In other words, Christ

reveals God to humanity and at the same time stands as the "new I" in whom all humanity participates. So the self, or I, is reconfigured christologically; Christ is the center of one's being or coming into being. Charles Marsh puts it another way: "Christ refashions the ontological structure of being itself such that all reality has Christ as its vital center."[9] In this way, each encounter between I and Other carries with it the possibility of presenting Christ to the Other or glimpsing Christ in the Other.

Bonhoeffer's concrete suggestions in *Life Together* (for life together) serve to illustrate how this presenting and glimpsing might be possible. The words of hymns sung in unison and the words of prayers offered communally tangibly unite congregations—made up of I's and Others—in the mediating Word of God. The act of breaking bread stands to remind each I and each Other that all are

beneficiaries of the sustenance and goodness that come from God, that all are united in spirit and body. In these activities Christ discloses an enduring relation of one to another. But Bonhoeffer's understanding of the relation between I and Other is more than a simple description of how individuals are to act with and toward one another; it is a model for the relation between an individual and community, between communities, and ultimately for the relation between God and humanity in general.

The conviction that the Other is not simply acknowledged but is someone with whom I share an inextricable bond is part of Bonhoeffer's unique contribution to the understanding of intersubjectivity—Christian intersubjectivity, in particular. It is the basis for a powerful incarnational theology. Bonhoeffer's description of the Christ-mediated, dialogical relation between I and Other underscores the primacy of human relation, affirms the integrity of the Other qua Other as *the* ethical benchmark for Christianity, and affirms inclusivity rather than exclusivity.

Bonhoeffer's rejection of Kantian notions about knowing, or reflecting, reality is important for his initial development of the idea that "Christ exists as community." But it also serves as a foundation for solving what Bonhoeffer calls the problem of act and being. The problem, or question, of act and being is age-old: should God's revelation be understood in such a way that God is always the one who acts, or in such a way that God is always the one who is? Historically, the answer always required a choice: act *or* being, one *or* the other, and, in brief, pitted existentialists against transcendentalists.

But Bonhoeffer works, particularly in *Act and Being*, to unify both themes as he interprets God's revelation to the world. Marsh helps us understand his argument, that revelation cannot be reduced to either act or being but "is a reality [that is] prior to both" and takes concrete form in "Christ existing as community."[10] Thus Bonhoeffer's solution to the problem of act and being is the church. The act-being question is simply a way of asking how we can know God. Bonhoeffer answers that we can know God in the church. His interpretation of revelation requires an ecclesiological form of thinking (*kirchliches Denken*) that recognizes the self-witness of God in the form of Jesus Christ, experienced in the social interactions of a church community. Revelation is encountered in the church; the church is the Christ of the present; it is "Christ existing as community."

In all the themes basic to Bonhoeffer's early theology—from the ethical concept of person (which is dependent on the claims the Other makes on me) to the possibility of an encounter with transcendence in human sociality—what is noted as remarkable is that "what is most essential to the self is found *outside itself*."[11] The life of discipleship is marked by being-with-others, and in this very being-with-others Christ is present. The ethical, anthropological, christological, theological, and ecclesiological meet in Bonhoeffer's iteration "Christ existing as community."

In the end for Bonhoeffer the call to discipleship—that costly call to follow after Christ—is inextricably tied to a profound sense of the suffering of Christ on behalf of others (and the suffering of those in whose midst one finds oneself). "Christ existing as community" is predicated on this understanding of suffering, in particular on the understanding that Christ "bore the sufferings of all humanity in his own body."[12] In entering into the sufferings of humanity, Christ creates community, the being-with-one-another and for-one-another. And this stands as the hallmark of Christian life and calls Christians—real persons in concrete,

historical locations—to do the same, that is, to live with one another and for one another, to bear the sufferings of the Other, in ethical (and christological) relation with the Other.

# CHAPTER THREE

## Costly Grace

Dietrich Bonhoeffer might be most widely and famously known for his conviction that grace is costly:

> Costly grace is the hidden treasure in the field, for the sake of which people go and sell with joy everything they have. . . . Costly grace is the gospel which must be sought again and again, the gift which has to be asked for, the door at which one has to knock. It is costly because it calls us to discipleship; it is grace, because it calls us to follow *Jesus Christ*. It is costly because it costs people their lives; it is grace, because it thereby makes them live. It is costly, because it condemns sin; it is grace, because it justifies the sinner. Above all, grace is costly, because it was costly to God, because it costs God the life of God's Son . . .

and because nothing can be cheap to us which is costly to God.[1]

Worked out in his book *Discipleship* (1937) and set in opposition to "cheap grace," "costly grace" is a rich concept grounded in the important philosophical work of Bonhoeffer's dissertations and foundational to his later thoughts in *Ethics* and *Letters and Papers from Prison*.

The first English translation of *Discipleship* sought to capture the importance of Bonhoeffer's ideas by titling the book *The Cost of Discipleship*. The new Dietrich Bonhoeffer Works in English (DBWE) edition of *Discipleship* offers a more direct translation of the German title *Nachfolge*, which can be literally rendered as "following after." It might be said that the whole of Bonhoeffer's life and theology are summed up in this simple understanding of discipleship as *following after* Christ. But discipleship cannot be fully comprehended apart from Bonhoeffer's key theological concepts already named: Christ existing as community, costly grace, vicarious representative action (*Stellvertretung*), ethics as formation, and religionless Christianity.

The concept of costly grace is rooted in Bonhoeffer's profound appreciation for Christ's redemptive suffering on behalf of humanity and in his understanding of Martin Luther's theology of the cross, doctrine of the two kingdoms, and interpretation of justification. In addition, the notion of costly grace echoes Bonhoeffer's thinking about pacifism, responsibility, and the relationship between faith and obedience. Finally, costly grace prefigures Bonhoeffer's later work on the "this-worldliness" of Christian faith.

As we have seen, Bonhoeffer wrote *Discipleship* during his tenure as director of Finkenwalde in 1935 and 1936, but his academic year at Union Theological Seminary in 1930–1931 was pivotal in shaping his views on discipleship.

Bonhoeffer's encounter with social ethicist Reinhold Niebuhr and his friendship with fellow student and pacifist Jean Lasserre were life changing. Niebuhr insisted on what may be called the unity of reality as well as a social interpretation of the gospel, while Lasserre asserted the Christian obligation to live out the Sermon on the Mount. These ideas were not new to Bonhoeffer, but his theological tradition, historical location, and formal German education kept him from immediately recognizing their value.

Theological inquiry and reflection, for Bonhoeffer, were distinct from concrete reality and activity in the world. Consequently, Bonhoeffer's initial resistance to Niebuhr's ideas about the necessary correlation between reflection and reality is not surprising. Niebuhr even described Bonhoeffer as apolitical and, along with Professor Eugene Lyman, pressed him to bring his academic insight, God's grace, and the needs of the world into conversation. In 1931, Bonhoeffer was not ready to make those connections.

For readers acquainted with Bonhoeffer's later political activism, this conflict with his Union professors may be unexpected. It is important to remember, however, that Bonhoeffer had been steeped in the Lutheran tradition of the two kingdoms. Luther maintained that although God rules the whole world, it is divided into two kingdoms: the earthly, secular kingdom on one hand, and the heavenly, spiritual kingdom on the other. Luther was attempting to articulate the relationship not only between church and state but between law and gospel as well, and he envisioned those relationships as dialectical in nature.

Luther never intended for the two kingdoms to be divided against one another. He certainly did not intend the distinction to be used as justification for the church's apathy and inaction in the "worldly" sphere. But that is precisely what had happened, especially by the time Bonhoeffer found himself facing the rising power of National Socialism and its all-encompassing ideology. German churches had adopted a "two-spheres" mentality that fostered a break between sacred activities (worship and the like) and secular responsibilities. Nazi abuse of the doctrine of two kingdoms to discourage church interference in affairs of the state forced Bonhoeffer to reexamine Luther's original understanding of the relationship between the sacred and the secular. It compelled him to recognize, in line with Niebuhr and Lyman, the inextricable relationship between theology and social responsibility. The importance of this correlation began to play itself out in the development of Bonhoeffer's notion of costly grace, though it reverberates through the rest of his life and work.

Bonhoeffer's friendship in New York with Jean Lasserre also proved significant for his thinking about costly grace. Lasserre was a committed pacifist who encouraged Bonhoeffer to consider the possibility that Jesus' Sermon on the Mount was neither an example (as in Lutheran circles) of the law writ large—impossible to fulfill and replete with reminders of humans' sinful nature—nor a hoped-for ideal possible to realize only at the end of time. Rather, Lasserre presented the Sermon as a series of commandments for living, here and now.

Blessed are the poor in spirit, for theirs is the kingdom of heaven.

Blessed are those who mourn, for they will be comforted.

Blessed are the meek, for they will inherit the earth.

Blessed are those who hunger and thirst for righteousness, for they will be filled.

Blessed are the merciful, for they will receive mercy.

Blessed are the pure in heart, for they will see God.

Blessed are the peacemakers, for they will be called children of God.

Blessed are those who are persecuted for righteousness' sake, for theirs is the kingdom of heaven.

Blessed are you when people revile you and persecute you and utter all kinds of evil against you falsely on my account. Rejoice and be glad, for your reward is great in heaven, for in the same way they persecuted the prophets who were before you. (Matt. 5:3–12)

In sermons preached during 1934 and 1935, as well as in *Discipleship*, Bonhoeffer wrestled with these verses, also known as the Beatitudes. With Lasserre's insight, his own appropriation of Luther's understanding of the doctrine of two kingdoms, and the solid foundation of his early work on the self-revelation of God in "Christ existing as community," Bonhoeffer concluded that the failure of the German churches to fight the villainous Nazi government had, in fact, cheapened the church and the grace it purported to offer. For Bonhoeffer the Sermon on the Mount stood as a profound and paradoxical call to faith in and obedience to Jesus Christ. The editors of *Discipleship* put it eloquently:

Bonhoeffer's emphasis on the obedient deeds of discipleship in response to God's word in Jesus Christ is in his view a restoration of the meaning of faith in a world that had become increasingly bereft of compassion, peace, forgiveness of enemies, purity of heart, and meekness, yet increasingly willing to exploit the poor and oppress those who struggle for justice. In short, the perspective of the Beatitudes of Jesus' Sermon on the Mount quickly became Bonhoeffer's way of elucidating the meaning of discipleship for Christians and their churches. If, in a nation that has turned away from Christianity, faith is ever to be restored, the church must preach again what is central in the Christian faith, the call of Jesus Christ to follow him.[2]

Following after is a costly affair, and it cost Bonhoeffer his life. His choice to suffer redemptively for others, after the fashion of Christ's redemptive suffering on behalf of the whole of humanity, marks his commitment to faith and obedience even unto death.

But Bonhoeffer's distinction between "cheap grace" and "costly grace" is more than a call to sacrificial action. It is a theological insight related to his understanding of Luther's doctrine of justification. At the most basic level, justification is about "getting right" with God. Anyone

who has ever typed a document on a computer (or even a typewriter) has thought about justification in this simple sense. If you select "left justify," the words are aligned on the left side of the page. "Right justify" lines up the words on the right side of the page. "Both justify" aligns the words with the margins on both sides of the paper (as with the text on this page). Christians are interested in being "lined up" with (or justified in the eyes of) God.

But justification is at once a very simple theological concept and one replete with historical nuance. In fact, to unpack fully Bonhoeffer's understanding of justification, it is necessary to consider the declarative interpretation of

justification (the classical Protestant doctrine articulated by Martin Luther) and the transformative doctrine of justification (the traditional Catholic position formulated by Augustine). Augustine and Luther agree that justification is possible only through God's gift of grace. They differ, however, on the nature of that gift. For Augustine, God's grace is a gift that transforms the recipient's thinking, willing, and believing so that he or she can love what God loves. The sinner, in Augustine's view, suffers from disordered loves; God's transformative gift of grace enables each person to reorder those loves and make God one's primary concern. God's forgiveness follows, but only in accord with one's own penitent and righteous actions. Augustine's biography sheds light on his interpretation of justification. His conversion to Christianity came late in his life, after a series of choices about which he was less than proud. (His most famous book is called *Confessions*!) He very much needed to change the way he was willing, thinking, believing, and acting. And he did so, with God's help.

As a young Augustinian monk, Martin Luther struggled with the concept of justification. He sought to understand it by wrestling with a verse in Paul's letter to the Romans that reads, "The one who is righteous will live by faith" (Rom. 1:17). Luther thought he had to be righteous before he could live by faith. To that end, he went to confession every day. But unlike Augustine he had very little to confess; he walked such a straight path that his frustrated confessor told him not to return until he had done something worth confessing. Not content, Luther studied theology and Scripture, particularly that problematic passage in Romans. His conclusion became a key component of the Protestant Reformation.

Luther came to understand righteousness—or justification—as a gift of unconditional mercy and forgiveness. In

Luther's view, sinful humans could never do enough or be enough to line themselves up with God. So Paul's assertion in Romans that "the one who is righteous will live by faith" describes righteousness as a generous gift from God. Accepting that gift, that grace, requires only a declaration of faith; hence the famous Lutheran dictum: justification (through grace) by faith alone.

Critics of Luther's declarative interpretation of justification charge that its adherents are simply lazy. If God's grace is sheer mercy and nothing one does can ever be adequate for salvation, why, they ask, do anything good at all? Conversely, Lutheran opponents of the traditionally Catholic transformative interpretation of justification fear that Christians must "earn" their salvation through "works righteousness" (thereby dismissing the saving acts of Jesus' death and resurrection).

Bonhoeffer acknowledges the potential of the Lutheran position to encourage lazy, even apathetic, Christians. Lutherans and other Protestant Christians who do not

recognize with James that faith without works is dead embrace what Bonhoeffer calls "cheap grace." But Bonhoeffer emphasizes that while the declarative position affirms the unconditional mercy of God's grace, it encourages, even requires, transformation. Bonhoeffer asserts, in fact, that those who think grace does not require discipleship misunderstand Luther.

Without abandoning Luther's basic affirmation that justification comes by faith alone, Bonhoeffer calls for an acknowledgment that grace is costly. "Costly grace . . . comes to us as a gracious call to follow Jesus; it comes as a forgiving word to the fearful spirit and the broken heart. Grace is costly, because it forces people under the yoke of following Jesus Christ; it is grace when Jesus says: 'My yoke is easy and my burden is light' (Matt. 11:30)."[3] With his notion of "costly grace," Bonhoeffer reasserts Luther's understanding of the link between grace and discipleship, while establishing a middle ground between the two classical versions of justification. It is a middle ground that anticipates the Joint Declaration of the Doctrine of Justification issued by the World Lutheran Federation and the Roman Catholic Church in 1999.

For Bonhoeffer, the crucial distinction between cheap and costly grace lies in the fact that costly grace acknowledges the correlation of grace and discipleship while cheap grace misses this correlation altogether. It is "the preaching of forgiveness without repentance . . . [it is] the Lord's Supper without confession of sin; it is absolution without personal confession." "Cheap grace," Bonhoeffer continues, "is grace without discipleship, grace without the cross, grace without the living, incarnate Jesus Christ." It is grace without the constant knowledge and hope of the life, death, and resurrection of Jesus Christ. It is "grace without the cross."[4]

Bonhoeffer goes so far as to say that cheap grace is the *mortal* enemy of the church: "Like ravens we have gathered around the carcass of cheap grace. From it we have imbibed the poison which has killed the following of Jesus among us."[5] It is also "that grace we bestow on ourselves."[6] It functions as a pass allowing the Christian to live in the same manner as before. Life under cheap grace, in fact, does not differ from life under sin; there is no following after Christ because cheap grace justifies the sin without transforming the sinner.

Bonhoeffer cannot emphasize strongly enough the unbreakable link between God's gift of grace and God's call to "follow after." Justification is a gift of grace, but it is not a gift that renders Christians free from responsibility. On the contrary, freedom from sin through (costly) grace makes possible the ability to follow Christ. In a way that prefigures the claims he will make in *Letters and Papers from Prison* about living a "this-worldly" life, Bonhoeffer reaffirms Luther's own appropriation of the doctrine of justification:

> Luther's deed cannot be misunderstood more grievously than by thinking that through discovering the gospel of pure grace, Luther proclaimed a dispensation from obeying Jesus' commandments in the world. The Reformation's main discovery would then be the sanctification and justification of the world by grace's forgiving power. For Luther, on the contrary, a Christian's secular vocation is justified only in that one's protest against the world is thereby most sharply expressed. A Christian's secular vocation receives new recognition from the gospel only to the extent that it is carried out while following Jesus. Luther's reason for leaving the monastery was not the justification of sin, but justification of the sinner. Costly grace was given as a gift to Luther. It was grace, because it was water onto thirsty land, comfort for anxiety, liberation from the servitude of a self-chosen path, forgiveness of all sins. The grace was costly, because it did not excuse one from works. Instead, it endlessly sharpened the call to discipleship.[7]

Those who level the harshest critique against Luther's doctrine of justification, Bonhoeffer would argue, are those who least understand it. They fail to recognize that for

Luther God's gracious gift of forgiveness meant that one must understand the call to discipleship more deeply and seriously than ever.

# CHAPTER FOUR

## *Stellvertretung* and Ethics as Formation

*Stellvertretung*, translated as "vicarious representative action," is a pivotal concept in Bonhoeffer's work from his first dissertation to his sermons, from his lifework *Ethics* (published posthumously) to the letters and papers written in prison. In this single term rests an effective summary of Bonhoeffer's understanding of Christ's suffering and death on behalf of all humanity and Christians' call to follow after Christ. *Stellvertretung*, most simply, is Bonhoeffer's description of how human beings are to be in the world. As Christ lived and died vicariously, his disciples are called to vicarious action and responsible love on behalf of the Other. In this idea, perhaps more than anywhere, the interrelated strands in Bonhoeffer's theological thinking are uncovered.

*Stellvertretung* as a thematic thread running through Bonhoeffer's work is tied inextricably to the secondary themes of freedom, responsibility, suffering, and faith's this-worldliness. These are, in turn, embedded in each of the primary themes: Christ existing as community, costly grace, ethics as formation, and religionless Christianity.

Thus Bonhoeffer's use of *Stellvertretung* cannot be understood apart from his claims about "Christ existing as community." The idea that God is revealed through the incarnate Christ in community is predicated on Christ's vicarious action on behalf of the community, as well as on the way that Christ's action enables each member of the community to act vicariously on behalf of the others. *Stellvertretung* makes meaningful Bonhoeffer's call to discipleship in the form of costly grace. It fosters understanding of Bonhoeffer's rejection of a formal ethic in favor of an ethic that is best described as conformation to Christ. And the concept of *Stellvertretung* is the foundation for Bonhoeffer's claims related to his religionless interpretation of Christianity, including the necessity of seeing the events of the world from the perspective of those who suffer. This perspective is what Bonhoeffer calls the "view from below."

Early English editions of Bonhoeffer's work translated *Stellvertretung* as "deputyship." But the concept of deputyship does not resonate with meaning for most English readers. The translation "vicarious representative action," used consistently in the Dietrich Bonhoeffer Works English editions, is more faithful to the meaning of the German word *Stellvertretung*. Much of the secondary literature, however—even reissued classics like Larry Rasmussen's *Dietrich Bonhoeffer: Reality and Resistance* (1972, 2005)—persists in using the language of "deputyship." And although Rasmussen has thorough notes explaining the word's connotations, otherwise rich sentences (e.g., "From Christ's sacrifice we recognize deputyship as the law of life for all men") lose their punch in translation.[1] The power of this sentence, and of Bonhoeffer's proposal that it is employed to explain, lies in the deep connections between Christ's sacrifice and *Stellvertretung*, both of which involve freedom and responsibility, vicarious action, and suffering. The language of vicarious representative action makes this correlation more poignant: from Christ's sacrifice we recognize vicarious representative action as the law of life for all people.

Note too the universality of this claim. In Bonhoeffer's early work, and even in *Discipleship, Stellvertretung* is located in the life and work of the church. But by the 1940s, when Bonhoeffer records the thoughts that would become *Ethics* and *Letters and Papers from Prison,* the concept has gained a moral component in addition to a theological one. It is no longer limited to the work of a Christian in the church community but refers to a way of being and acting in the world applicable to all people—a way that, in fact, defines one's humanity. In a beautiful twist on the classical theological dictum that God became human so that humans might become divine, Bonhoeffer argues that God became human so that humans could become truly human.[2]

The concept of *Stellvertretung* permeates all Bonhoeffer's work, highlighting the consistent christological center of his thinking. The Christ-centered, or "christocentric," nature of Bonhoeffer's thought is clear when we note how consistently he asks the questions "Who is Jesus Christ?" and "Who is Jesus Christ for us today?" These questions are implied in *Sanctorum Communio* in 1927, addressed directly in Bonhoeffer's lectures on Christology in 1933, foundational to his *Ethics* in the 1940s, and revisited in his

letters from prison in 1944. "The one who is present in word, sacrament, and community," proclaims Bonhoeffer, "is the center of human existence, history, and nature. It is part of the structure of his person that he stands center."[3]

Bonhoeffer's Christology is rooted in a deep appreciation of Luther's theology of the cross—that is, the conviction that the fullness of God is revealed in the humanity of Jesus, in his sacrificial death, and resurrection. This particular christological lens makes it possible to understand Bonhoeffer's affirmation, following Luther, that the freedom which comes by way of the cross is not a freedom *from* but a freedom *to*. It is not freedom from responsibility or license to act on one's every whim but freedom to serve the neighbor and the world. This christocentric view of freedom as suffering service is at the very heart of Bonhoeffer's ethics, which is shaped by a Lutheran theology of the cross.

Bonhoeffer envisioned *Ethics* as his magnum opus. And despite the fact that it was not finished when he died and that the intended order of the extant material is not certain, most scholars regard it as such. The power of the text derives, in large part, from its rootedness in a real and burning question: What constitutes responsible Christian action in the world? In the context of Nazi Germany's "Final Solution" this was quite literally a question of life and death. Bonhoeffer wrote out of this context, and he

wrote to answer this question. He did not write *Ethics* as an academic exercise in abstraction and speculation. For him the future of the church, of Germany, and even of Christianity and humanity per se were at stake.

The history of ethical theory is long and storied. But established ethical frameworks—whether dependent on reason, moral principles, or virtue—Bonhoeffer viewed as inadequate foundations for an ethic of responsible action. In this sense Bonhoeffer's work represents a departure from previous ethical formulations. He hints at this departure in a well-known passage in the essay "After Ten Years," given to and in support of his co-conspirators at the turn of the new year 1943:

> Who stands fast? Only the man whose final standard is not his reason, his principles, his conscience, his freedom, or his virtue, but who is ready to sacrifice all this when he is called to obedient and responsible action in faith and in exclusive allegiance to God— the responsible man, who tries to make his whole life an answer to the question and call of God.[4]

Theologian John de Gruchy clarifies the point of this passage in the outstanding documentary *Bonhoeffer* (2003): " 'What does it mean to do good?' is the wrong [ethical] question for Bonhoeffer. The right one, anachronistic as it might seem, is 'What is the will of God?' "[5] In other words, de Gruchy claims, the real question is what is it that, at this moment of our lives, we are required to do?

Wondering about the will of God and its implications for living in the face of a blatantly evil government makes sense in light of Bonhoeffer's theology, Christology, and soteriology (understanding of salvation), all of which are foundational for his ethics. In the incarnation of Jesus,

Bonhoeffer argues, God is reconciled to all humanity and all humanity is reconciled to God. This reconciliation through Christ forms a new ontological reality. It gives rise, in fact, to a new humanity—a claim present in the earliest of Bonhoeffer's works, *Sanctorum Communio*—and introduces the notion of conformation to Christ that undergirds Bonhoeffer's ethic of free and responsible action.

Bonhoeffer is careful to say that what he means by "formation" or "conformation" is most likely quite different from what one might assume. "Formation occurs only by being drawn into the form of Jesus Christ, by *being conformed to the unique form of the one who became human, was crucified, and is risen*."[6] Conformation to Christ does not require that Christians try to emulate Jesus in their every action; it is not the formulaic "What would Jesus do?" Conformation to Christ does not establish patterns of

behavior or action in the world that are universally valid. But conformation to Christ does make human beings more fully human and free—to stand in judgment, to accept grace, to be united with Christ in love and in community:

> To be conformed to the one who has become human—that is what being human really means . . . to be conformed to the crucified—that means to be a human being judged by God . . . to be conformed to the risen one—that means to be a new human being before God . . . [to be conformed to Christ means] Jesus Christ taking form in Christ's church. The New Testament, in deep and clear indication of the matter itself, calls the church the body of Christ.[7]

Bonhoeffer's point is, in the end, a simple one. Christ is not a principle or program; Christ does not teach an abstract ethic. Rather, Christ was really and concretely human, committed to serving the needs of real humans in specific situations. And as Bonhoeffer's situation was certainly specific, his context, as he writes, is ever present. The war, the vilification and annihilation of Jews and others, the co-opting of the church by proponents of Nazi ideology—all this required ethical action on the part of Christians. But the choices were difficult. Bonhoeffer's understanding of ethics as formation opens possibilities for acting freely, responsibly, and obediently, but often at great personal cost.

Bonhoeffer's call to ethical and responsible action remains costly. Ethics as formation, grounded in his understanding of *Stellvertretung*, requires a willingness—as part of conformation to Christ—to suffer or take on guilt. Bonhoeffer acknowledges that in some situations responsible action carried out in faith and in obedience to God—for example, killing a tyrant—may be sinful action. In those cases, one must depend on a God who demands such action but who "promises forgiveness and consolation" to the one who becomes a sinner in the process.[8]

Bonhoeffer's context demanded that he rethink traditional approaches to ethical decision making; his theology, particularly his Christology and radical understanding of grace, allowed him to do so. Consequently, *Ethics* is marked not only by a description of ethics as formation, or conformation to Christ, but by a number of significant shifts: Bonhoeffer argues for a unity of reality in lieu of the traditional (pseudo-Lutheran) doctrine of two kingdoms; he abandons the traditionally articulated structure of "orders of creation" in favor of ethical mandates; and he places a premium on the importance of the penultimate in relationship to the ultimate.

The doctrine of two kingdoms divides reality into

realms—an earthly, secular kingdom on the one hand and a spiritual and heavenly kingdom on the other. Precipitated by the Reformation's rejection of papal authority, the distinction was subsequently etched in sharper lines than Martin Luther envisioned. In Luther's estimation, the kingdoms existed in relationship to one another and were both ruled by God. But in practical applications of the doctrine, especially in Nazi Germany, the distinction was employed as a way of claiming two distinct and independent realms in which God's will could be revealed. Bonhoeffer's christological redescription of humanity and the world, beginning in his earliest work, compelled him to reject two-realms thinking: "There are not two realities, but *only one reality*, and that is God's reality revealed in Christ in the reality of the world. . . . It is a denial of God's revelation in Jesus Christ to wish to be 'Christian' without being 'worldly,' or [to] wish to be worldly without seeing and recognizing the world in Christ."[9] Bonhoeffer's embrace of this unitary view of reality was undoubtedly influenced by American theologian Reinhold Niebuhr (despite Bonhoeffer's initial resistance to Niebuhr's ideas) and was developed further in his concept of religionless Christianity in *Letters and Papers from Prison*.

In the economic and political turmoil of Germany in the 1930s, the prevailing ethics were based on orders of creation that provided people a desperately desired sense of security. According to this approach, God's command for ethical action could be discovered in created "orders" such as family, nation, and *Volk*. But Bonhoeffer was wary. Even before Nazi-sympathizing Christians co-opted the orders of creation to justify nationalist and racist policies as natural expressions of a God-willed Germandom, Bonhoeffer recognized just this possibility. The orders of creation, he realized, could be used to baptize most any position or prejudice; in effect they afforded theological credibility to ideological constructions. In *Ethics*, over against both the orders of creation and the two-kingdoms doctrine, Bonhoeffer proposed four divine "mandates" corresponding to the traditional "orders" of marriage and family, work, church, and state. For Bonhoeffer, the purpose of the mandates was to help preserve life and order the world.

Two salient features of the mandates served to protect them from the perils of "orders of creation": mandates are commanded by God and ordered toward Christ. These conditions mean that the mandates cannot be identified with particular historical forms (administrations or family structures). Because any number of historical particularities may fulfill the divine call, emphasis falls on God rather than the worldly structures themselves. Furthermore, the mandates echo Bonhoeffer's embrace of the unity of reality and long-standing commitments to living with and for the

Other, for to order the world toward Christ is to overturn thinking that divides reality into two realms. Participation in the world by way of family, work, church, and state is, in Bonhoeffer's view, participation in the reality of Christ *today*.

In a similar vein, Bonhoeffer seeks to clarify the important relationship between the ultimate and the penultimate, or between last things and things before the last things. The penultimate does not serve as a precondition for the ultimate; rather, the ultimate determines the penultimate. But it does so in a way that respects the integrity of the penultimate and requires Christians to take seriously matters of the world. Christ himself breaks into the world and demands care of it. The incarnation and resurrection transform the old humanity into the new. Grace and justification—pronouncements of the ultimate—compel the new humanity into action. Thus, a hungry child needs bread as much as she needs the words of redemption. Bonhoeffer is clear on this point: "For the sake of the ultimate the penultimate must be preserved."[10] The Christian, conformed to Christ, acts and suffers on behalf of those in *this* world.

## CHAPTER FIVE

# Religionless Christianity

At first blush, Bonhoeffer's *Letters and Papers from Prison* may appear to be a collection of quaint notes exchanged with his family in which Bonhoeffer requests books and clean pants while downplaying the bleakness of his living conditions. But this collection of letters from his cell in the military interrogation prison at Berlin-Tegel includes correspondence with Bonhoeffer's best friend and theological confidant, Eberhard Bethge, in which he ruminates on various theological issues, including "religionless Christianity." This concept, built on his previous claims about community and grace, freedom and responsible action, is the culmination of his theological thinking. In short, Bonhoeffer's articulation of religionless Christianity is a powerful redescription of Christ as the coming of God into the world.

The text of section 3 of *Letters and Papers from Prison* (which includes letters dated between April and July 1944) and selected documents from section 4 are critical for unpacking Bonhoeffer's concept of religionless Christianity. In April 1944, after one year in prison, Bonhoeffer asks Bethge, "How can Christ become the Lord of the religionless? Are there religionless Christians?"[1] Implicit in these questions are Bonhoeffer's conviction that he is living in a "world come of age"—a religionless time—and his concern with understanding Christ *today*. How, he wondered, in a secular, religionless, come-of-age world do we construe Christianity, justification, repentance, and faith? Bonhoeffer's letters to Bethge indicate that he wants to reinterpret faith as well as its central theological concepts in order to develop a "this-worldly Christianity":

> What is bothering me incessantly is the question what Christianity really is, or indeed who Christ really is, for us today. The time when people could be told everything by means of words, whether theological or pious, is over, and so is the time of inwardness and conscience—and that means the time of religion in general. We are moving towards a completely religionless time; people as they are now simply cannot be religious any more.[2]

What Bonhoeffer means, or hopes to achieve, by interpreting Christianity for a "completely religionless time" is not immediately evident. If our question is Bonhoeffer's question—"What, then, is religionless Christianity?"—part of

the challenge is piecing together the fragments of his answer scattered throughout various prison letters.

As he continues to work out the solution for himself, Bonhoeffer asks the question this way: "If religion is only a garment of Christianity—and even this garment has looked different at different times—then what is a religionless Christianity?"[3] Bonhoeffer wants to strip Christianity of all but its barest essentials in order to discover its heart, or core. In a world that no longer sees religion as its starting point for self-understanding, what is Christianity

121

beyond the manifestations of religion that change over time? Based on his fragmentary answers to this question, we can say two things: First, the conclusions Bonhoeffer draws about religionless Christianity are claims about Christ as Lord of the world, claims that simultaneously speak about love, suffering, and responsible action. Second, the key to understanding these claims is uncovering what Bonhoeffer means by *deus ex machina*, "world come of age," *etsi deus non daretur*, and faith.

## Deus Ex Machina

"Religious people speak of God," writes Bonhoeffer, "when human knowledge (perhaps simply because they are too lazy to think) has come to an end, or when human resources fail—in fact, it is always the *deus ex machina* that they bring on to the scene, either for the apparent solution of insoluble problems, or as strength in human failure."[4] Bonhoeffer is distressed by the fact that God has come to be known primarily as one who answers unanswerable questions—one who waits in the wings, on the boundaries of life, to be ushered in during times of human impotence. From Bonhoeffer's view, this is an inappropriate, even dangerous, image of God.

*Deus ex machina* ("god from the machine") is a term from ancient Greek and Roman theater. When characters faced irresolvable conflicts, a divine character dropped onto the stage by wires attached to pulleys (i.e., "the machine"), resolved the conflict, and exited as swiftly and mysteriously as he or she had entered. For many (so-called) religious people, Bonhoeffer contends, God functions in precisely this way. But God, in this role, must remain forever on the boundaries of human life and experience. Because humans find themselves increasingly able to answer questions on

their own—through scientific advancement, or existential and psychological analysis—they are increasingly able to understand the world and themselves without recourse to God. Consequently, this God (or this image of God as *deus ex machina*) steadily becomes superfluous.

In discussing the possibility of a "religionless Christianity," then, Bonhoeffer is interested in rethinking the place, image, and role of God in modern life. "I should like to speak of God not on the boundaries but at the center, not in weaknesses but in strength; and therefore not in death and guilt but in man's life and goodness," he writes.[5] Bonhoeffer's thinking here reflects a rereading of the New Testament with a concomitant appraisal of God's self-revelation in Jesus as the Christ who comes into the world to live among people, especially the weak and suffering.

123

## World Come of Age

In May 1944, Bonhoeffer wrote to Bethge that he had been reading Carl Friedrich von Weizäcker's book *The World-View of Physics*. It reinforces, he says, that using God as a stopgap or a *deus ex machina* is wrong. The physicist helps Bonhoeffer recognize that the frontiers of knowledge are ever expanding and that for some God is continually pushed back with those changing boundaries. With this in mind, Bonhoeffer argues that God should not be sought only in unsolved problems, in what is unknown; God, he says, is to be found in what we know, in the center of our lives and not at the boundaries.

For Bonhoeffer, finding God in what we know means that Christians do not have to fear scientific knowledge. Scientific progress does not and should not affect our understanding of or relationship with God. Bonhoeffer recognizes that this is true for other realms of knowledge

as well. "God wants us to realize his presence, not in unsolved problems but in those that are solved. . . . It is true of the wider human problems of death, suffering, and guilt."[6] Even in these boundary situations, says Bonhoeffer, it is possible to find answers without recourse to God. Because more and more people do so, a God who is understood only as a source of answers to unanswered questions is no answer at all, even to questions (about death and suffering, for example) traditionally reserved for God.

In another letter, Bonhoeffer writes that

> God must be recognized at the center of life, not when we are at the end of our resources; it is his will to be recognized in life, and not only when death comes; in health and vigour, and not only in suffering; in our activities, and not only in sin. *The ground for this lies in the revelation of God in Jesus Christ*. He is the centre of life, and he certainly didn't "come" to answer our unsolved problems.[7]

Recognizing God at the center of life does three things for Bonhoeffer: it discloses the problematic nature of the common understanding of God as a stopgap or *deus ex machina*, it exposes the extent to which the world has "come of age," and it shows how the biblical concept of God—the revelation of God in Jesus Christ—opens the way to compassionate action in the world on behalf of others.

Thus Christ as the self-revelation of God—as the center of life—is critical to understanding Bonhoeffer's conception of religionless Christianity, and this conception participates in the christological center of his theology. It would be difficult to overemphasize the role of Christ in the whole of Bonhoeffer's work. It would be equally difficult to overstate the centrality of Christ here, especially at this juncture.

So what does Bonhoeffer mean by the strange formulation "world come of age"? He observes that the move toward human autonomy, from the thirteenth century on, has reached completion. In every realm of knowledge—from science to social and political matters, from art to ethics and religion—"man has learnt to deal with himself in all questions of importance without recourse to the 'working hypothesis' called 'God.' "[8] It is in this sense that we live in a world come of age. Even in the realms of ethics and religion, even with regard to ultimate questions historically reserved for theology, the world has become aware that it is possible to answer those questions without recourse to God.

## Etsi Deus non Daretur

Again and again, Bonhoeffer reiterates that in a world come of age God as a working hypothesis, as an answer to unanswerable questions, has been abolished. And where this hypothesis has not been abolished, it needs to be. We are called to live in the world, Bonhoeffer says, *etsi deus non daretur*—as if there were no God. For many early interpreters of Bonhoeffer this claim and his entire discussion of religionless Christianity was misunderstood, even misappropriated. Several 1960s death-of-God theologians, for instance, claimed Bonhoeffer as one of their own. But they missed Bonhoeffer's point:

> So our coming of age leads us to a true recognition of our situation before God. God would have us know that we must live as men [and women] who manage our lives without him. The God who is with us is the God who forsakes us (Mark 15.34). The God who lets us live in the world without the working hypothesis of God is the God before whom we stand continually. Before God and with God we live without God.[9]

In a world come of age we live without the false conception of God as a working hypothesis; we live without the concept of God as *deus ex machina*. But doing so opens the way to seeing God as God chooses to reveal himself in the biblical story, in Jesus as the Christ. In this view, Christ is in the center of life and not at the boundaries of our experience.

This reclaimed understanding of Christ is the good news of religionless Christianity. It is the good news of Jesus on the cross: Christ is with us and helps us, Bonhoeffer claims, not by power and omnipotence but by weakness and suffering. The one who is pushed out of the world and onto the cross is the one who is with us in our suffering. For Bonhoeffer, the difference between the *deus ex machina* God and the suffering Christ marks the difference between religion and Christianity. Bonhoeffer expresses the difference this way: "Man's religiosity makes him look in his distress to the power of God in the world: God is the *deus ex machina*. The Bible directs man to God's power-lessness and suffering: only the suffering God can help."[10]

To live in this world and share in the suffering of God is the call of each Christian, says Bonhoeffer. It is a call to live a "secular life." No one is called or obliged to be *religious* in a particular way. But each one is called to follow after Christ, to participate in this life. In his famous essay "After Ten Years," written as moral support for his coconspirators at the ten-year mark of Hitler's reign, and published in *Letters and Papers from Prison*, Bonhoeffer emphatically notes

that this world must not be dismissed out of hand. His point is to distinguish between those who count themselves religious and, in pious escapism, do nothing in the face of Nazi atrocities, and those who choose to embrace their responsibilities in the real and secular world, acting out their faith on behalf of future generations.

## Faith

Faith, for Bonhoeffer, is something whole. It stands in contrast to religion or the religious act, which is something partial:

> [A Christian] must live a "secular" life, and thereby share in God's sufferings. He *may* live a "secular" life (as one who has been freed from false religious obligations and inhibitions). To be a Christian does not mean to be religious in a particular way, to make something of oneself (a sinner, a penitent, or a saint) on the basis of some method or other, but to be a man—not a type of man, but the man that Christ creates in us. It is not the religious act that makes the Christian, but participation in the sufferings of God in the secular life. That is *metanoia* [transformation]: not in the first place thinking about one's own needs, problems, sins, and fears, but allowing oneself to be caught up into the way of Jesus Christ, into the messianic event. . . . The "religious act" is always something partial; "faith" is something whole, involving the whole of one's life. Jesus calls men, not to a new religion, but to life.[11]

On July 21, 1944, the day after the conspirators' final unsuccessful attempt on Hitler's life, Bonhoeffer resumed his reflections on the meaning of Christianity in a world

come of age. He wrote to Bethge that he had come to know and to understand, more and more, the "this-worldliness of Christianity."[12] He does not speak of "this-worldliness" in a superficial sense. It is not, he says, the "shallow and banal this-worldliness of the enlightened, the busy, the comfortable, or the lascivious," but, rather, a profound this-worldliness. "Religionless Christianity" is this-worldly in a way that is "characterized by discipline and the constant knowledge of death and resurrection."[13]

In this same letter, Bonhoeffer recalls his friendship with Jean Lasserre, the French student at Union Theological Seminary, and the deep and lasting impact Lasserre had on him. Lasserre, he recollects, hoped to become a saint. "I think it's quite likely that he did become one," muses Bonhoeffer.[14] He also recalls that he, himself, had a different goal. "At the time," he writes, "I was very impressed [with Lasserre], but I disagreed with him, and said, in effect, that I should like to learn to have faith. For a long time, I didn't realize the depth of the contrast. I thought I could acquire faith by trying to live a holy life, or something like it."[15] But faith, Bonhoeffer explains, comes simply and only by living completely and unreservedly in this world, in its duties, problems, successes, failures, experiences, and perplexities.[16]

The theme is familiar by now. We find God at the center of our experience, not at the boundaries being pushed ever farther away. Christianity is this-worldly in this sense: here, in this world, "we throw ourselves into the arms of God, taking seriously, not our own sufferings, but those of God in the world—watching with Christ in Gethsemane."[17] Faith is not the religious act; it is not something partial. Rather, faith is always whole. It is the whole of one's life:

"Jesus calls men [and women], not to a new religion, but to life."[18]

Bonhoeffer's conception of Christianity as nothing less than the sharing of God's sufferings in the world—sharing in the sufferings of all those Others who meet us, make an ethical claim on us, demand a response from us—*is* the culmination of his life's work. In fact, the power of *Letters and Papers from Prison* lies, in part, in the fact that it is continuous with Bonhoeffer's earlier thinking, particularly his christological thinking.

Responsible action, undertaken in the spirit of love and on behalf of others, especially others who are suffering, is an image of Christ consistent with the one presented in *Sanctorum Communio*, in his Christology lectures and sermons, in *Discipleship*, and in *Ethics*. From his earliest manuscript, where "Christ existing as community" places Christ as the important *between* that bridges each I and each Other, Christ is at the center of Bonhoeffer's theology. And true *following after* requires the willingness to love Others enough to suffer alongside them, to suffer for them, even to assume guilt on their behalf. Vicarious representative action (*Stellvertretung*) can be quite costly.

## Christians and Pagans

In a prison poem titled "Christians and Pagans" Bonhoeffer expresses with great poignancy the general themes of religionless Christianity. "In its own brief, poetic way," write Geffrey Kelly and Burton Nelson, "this poem is a summary of Bonhoeffer's understanding of the essence of one's relationship with God":[19]

All go to God in their distress,
Seek help and pray for bread and happiness,

Deliverance from pain, guilt and death.
All do, Christians and others.

All go to God in His distress,
Find him poor, reviled without shelter or bread,
Watch him tormented by sin, weakness, and death.
Christians stand by God in His agony.

God goes to all in their distress,
Satisfies body and soul with His bread,
Dies, crucified for all, Christians and others,
And both alike forgiving.[20]

The first stanza of this poem paints an image of those who perceive God as the *deus ex machina*. God is useful; God is God for *my* needs. God is summoned when I am in trouble. The second stanza portrays God in the world, weak and suffering: "poor, reviled without shelter or bread." The image is bleak; Bonhoeffer's language is strong. "Tormented" is God; whelmed by the wicked, the ones who cause others to suffer, by the weak, and by the dead. This picture reflects Bonhoeffer's revisioning of the biblical concept of God. Rejecting God as the one who is called on in times of need and trouble, it illuminates a God who enters into the pain and suffering of the world.

The last line of the second stanza points simultaneously to the image of Jesus in the garden at Gethsemane preparing to bear the weight of human suffering on his shoulders, and the Christians who stand by him and understand that to follow Christ is to shoulder some of that weight. This sharing in the sufferings of God in the world is discipleship; it is costly grace; it is "this-worldly Christianity." In Bonhoeffer's words to Bethge, it is "the profound this-worldliness, characterized by . . . the constant knowledge of death and resurrection."[21]

The poem's third stanza cuts to the core of Bonhoeffer's theological and ontological understanding of the Other. God goes to "all." For Christians and pagans *alike*, he hangs dead. He forgives all. Bonhoeffer posits no conditions or exclusionary clauses. The Other is, indeed, a fixed ontological marker of divine grace. Bonhoeffer's fundamental, christologically centered position regarding the status of the Other (and the salvific efficacy of the life, death, and resurrection of Jesus Christ) remains unchanged.

John Matthews offers a retelling of this poem in lyric form. "Christians, like all others, loved by God who hangs there dead. / Offering, forgiving, sacrificing in their stead."[22]

This is Matthews's rendering of the crucial lines in the third stanza of the original poem, lines that speak to the vicarious suffering Christ undertakes on behalf of all humanity. Exercising poetic license, Matthews adds a fourth stanza that underscores the uniqueness of Christian identity, discipleship, and vocation as Bonhoeffer presents it: "Lord, help us to look for you in those who are bestead, / In the lives of broken people, seeking peace and bread. / Where you are we wish to meet you, strengthen us, O Lord, / To be Christ for others, bringing water and the Word."[23]

Bonhoeffer, in this poem, is continuing to think, or rethink, answers to the question he first posed to Bethge on April 30, 1944: "What is bothering me incessantly is the question what Christianity really is, or indeed who Christ really is, for us today."[24] Matthews's verses are explicit.

Christianity really is about being "loved by God who hangs there dead" (on behalf of Christians and all others alike). Christ is found *today* in "our poor, neglected neighbors[,] . . . in the lives of broken people."[25] Christians stand by God as they share in God's sufferings as Jesus did.

## Outline of a Book

"Christians and Pagans" is not the only text in *Letters and Papers from Prison* that is animated by Bonhoeffer's understanding of religionless Christianity. In his prison notes from July–August 1944 is the outline of a book, which he proposes to be divided into three sections: "A Stocktaking of Christianity," "The Real Meaning of Christianity," and "Conclusions." This outline is his attempt to order the fragmented thoughts in his letters to Bethge between April and July 1944. Bonhoeffer's remarks for each section are brief but notably comprehensive.

In his comments for the first section, Bonhoeffer reiterates that God as a "working hypothesis, as a stop-gap for our embarrassments, has become superfluous."[26] But for our purposes the second and third sections are most relevant. Bonhoeffer's plans for the second chapter include addressing the question "Who is God?" His answer, as I have suggested, goes to the heart of "religionless Christianity." God's presence in and suffering in this world are inextricably tied to his nonreligious interpretation of Christianity. In a well-known passage, he writes:

> Who is God? Not in the first place an abstract belief in God, in his omnipotence, etc. That is not a genuine experience of God, but a partial extension of the world. Encounter with Jesus Christ. The experience that a transformation of all human life is given in the

fact that *"Jesus is there only for others."* His "being there for others" is the experience of transcendence. It is only this "being there for others," maintained till death, that is the ground of his omnipotence, omniscience, and omnipresence. Faith is participation in this being of Jesus (incarnation, cross, and resurrection). . . . *Our relation to God is a new life in "existence for others," through participation in the being of Jesus.* The transcendental is not infinite and unattainable tasks, but the neighbor who is within reach of any given situation.[27]

God's presence in the world, God's weakness in the world, are the only means by which God wins space and power in the world. "The transcendental is not infinite and unattainable tasks, but the neighbor." Geffrey Kelly and Burton

Nelson comment that "this for Bonhoeffer is the decisive difference between religion that feeds on a sense of power and Christianity that affirms God's strength in weakness as God suffers in the world."[28]

The third section of Bonhoeffer's book proposal revisits his commitment to the sociality of theology. "The church is the church only when it exists for others."[29] He continues by stating that the "church must share in the secular problems of ordinary human life, not dominating, but helping and serving. It must tell men of every calling what it means to live in Christ, *to exist for others*."[30]

The words of Bonhoeffer's July 21, 1944, letter to Bethge resound with his realization of "the profound this-worldliness of Christianity": "I discovered . . . that it is only by living completely in this world that one learns to have faith."[31] By this-worldliness, he continues, "I mean living unreservedly in life's duties, problems, successes, failures, experiences and perplexities."[32] In doing so, says Bonhoeffer, we take seriously the sufferings of God in the world. We can and we do watch with Christ in Gethsemane.

# CHAPTER SIX

## Legacy

As we hope readers have discovered in the previous chapters, Bonhoeffer's theology is both profound and relevant, philosophically sophisticated and grounded in concrete existence. But in the years immediately following his death, some of Bonhoeffer's admirers wondered whether this great Christian also qualified as a great theologian. Today it would be difficult to find anyone who shares this concern, for in recent decades appreciation for Bonhoeffer as a thinker has steadily grown. If Bonhoeffer first seized the attention of theologians with the fragmentary musings of *Letters and Papers from Prison*, he has maintained that attention because systematic works such as *Sanctorum Communio*, *Act and Being*, *Christ the Center*, and *Ethics* reveal the originality, consistency, and depth of his thought. Add to this the wide popularity of texts from his Finkenwalde period—*Discipleship* and *Life Together*—and Bonhoeffer's influence as a Christian theologian should not be in question.

Nor has the consensus that Bonhoeffer was an important theologian done anything to diminish his reputation as a great Christian. In fact, Bonhoeffer's unique place in the Christian imagination reflects the unique symbiosis he was able to achieve between life and thought. Many readers will be familiar with the success of Martin Doblmeier's documentary film *Bonhoeffer* (2003), which explores the theologian's insights and chronicles his heroic resistance to Hitler. But most will not be aware that this is only the most recent of a dozen or so documentary and dramatic films that explore Bonhoeffer's life. Nor should we ignore the many other ways Bonhoeffer's influence is evident beyond the halls of academe—from monuments bearing his likeness in the United States, Germany, Poland, and the United Kingdom, to streets, hospitals, and hotels named in his honor, paintings and musical arrangements that celebrate his legacy, stage plays that highlight his internal struggles, biographies written for lay audiences, historical novels in which he appears as a character, and devotional texts compiled from his writings. While these works vary in accuracy and quality, each testifies to a persistent fascination with Bonhoeffer's life and thought, as well as the connections between them.

Another feature of Bonhoeffer's reception that distinguishes him in the landscape of contemporary theology is the broad diversity of interpretations that are applied to him. Without doubt, the legacy of many an influential thinker has been claimed by competing interpretive "schools." But in Bonhoeffer's case we are dealing with more than contending scholarly analyses, more than differences of theological perspective; we have, in a very real sense, different Bonhoeffers.[1]

## Which Bonhoeffer?

During the past forty years, Bonhoeffer has been claimed by interpreters across the spectrum of contemporary religious thought. The decade of the 1960s gave us a Marxist Bonhoeffer compatible with East German socialism as well as an atheistic Bonhoeffer fashioned in the image of Anglo-American death-of-God theologians. The antiwar Bonhoeffer of the 1970s opposed American involvement in Vietnam, while during the 1980s Bonhoeffer became a progenitor of Latin American liberation theology and a theological antidote to the easy pieties of the Reagan-Bush era. During the same decade, Bonhoeffer began to be

portrayed as a friend of Jews whose theology represented a basis for post-Holocaust Christian-Jewish reconciliation.

On the theological right, the response to Bonhoeffer was initially cautious. But by the 1990s many conservative Christians were embracing a Bonhoeffer who seemed committed to evangelical values. Given the extent and diversity of American evangelicalism, it is not surprising that Bonhoeffer performs many roles within the movement. For some he is a culture warrior whose opposition to his own government's assault on innocent life inspires Christians to actively oppose abortion. For others he is a "critical patriot" who convicts American Christians of their captivity to nationalism, militarism, and empire. Still other evangelicals see Bonhoeffer as an ecclesiological innovator who can serve as a guide for the "emerging church."

Bonhoeffer's popularity continues to spread, even among those who are not traditionally religious. Many, admiring Bonhoeffer's bravery but put off by the "sectarian" concerns of Christian theology, are attracted to a man they believe personifies the universal values of courage and compassion. Pundits invoke him in a myriad of competing causes. This was particularly evident in the aftermath of 9/11, when Bonhoeffer was featured in arguments on both sides of the Bush administration's "war on terror." Hawks saw in Bonhoeffer a justification for preemptive military force, while doves emphasized his pacifism and portrayed his turn to violence as a desperate last resort.

Few if any historical figures have come to mean so many different things to so many different people. For scholars, the natural response to this plethora of competing interpretations is to hold up the *real* Bonhoeffer—that is, the Bonhoeffer of history rather than of imagination—as a measure of their legitimacy. It is certainly true that Bonhoeffer's voice will respond to the call of the careful researcher. But it can be very difficult for the average reader to distinguish this voice in the welter of claims being made for Bonhoeffer in the twenty-first century.

## The Search for Validity

The absence of a single authorized version of Bonhoeffer's life and legacy should not keep us from identifying a range of valid perspectives. No interpretation of Bonhoeffer is likely to achieve consensus, but we can begin to judge the validity of a given portrait of the man by asking the questions that follow.

*Is it informed by the entire scope of his life?* If the focus rests too narrowly on the Bonhoeffer of the church struggle, or the Bonhoeffer of Finkenwalde, or the prison

Bonhoeffer, one risks mistaking a snapshot of the man for a developed portrayal.

*Does it place his life in its proper contexts?* Eberhard Bethge's definitive biography is indispensible for viewing Bonhoeffer in the contexts of German society and the German church.

*Is it informed by the best scholarship?* The publication of Dietrich Bonhoeffer Works in English (DBWE) has made it possible for nonspecialists with the time and inclination to study original texts illuminated by thorough research.

*Does it attend to the continuities in Bonhoeffer's thought over time?* There has been considerable disagreement since the 1950s over the extent of this continuity. In part because of the bold and lonely steps Bonhoeffer took in ecclesiastical and political resistance, in part because of provocative statements in his prison letters, many have concluded that the crucible of anti-Nazi resistance utterly reshaped this child of bourgeois privilege. But close attention to his early writings—particularly his letters, sermons, and student papers—reveals that after age eighteen Bonhoeffer's basic theological outlook remained fairly consistent. Any interpretation of Bonhoeffer that does not acknowledge this continuity is doomed to distortion.

*Does it portray Bonhoeffer as a pastor-theologian?* In the view of many scholars, Bonhoeffer's significance is tied to the ways he was able to balance his training as an academic theologian with his commitment to pastoral work. He did not relate these worlds as a failed academic or a faithless priest. His unique vocational path was forged not in weakness or confusion but in strength and vision. Without forsaking his interest in theology he devoted himself to campus ministry, confirmation, preaching, and the training of seminarians. Any valid picture of Bonhoeffer will communicate his dual vocation of pastor and scholar.

*Does it acknowledge his penchant for crossing boundaries?*
Particularly in comparison with his contemporaries in post–
World War I Germany, Bonhoeffer demonstrated an
unusual willingness to cross cultural, ethnic, and economic
boundaries. These included the international frontiers he
traversed in travels to Rome, North Africa, Barcelona, New
York, Mexico, and Cuba, but also the social boundaries he
transgressed in repeated passages between the Upper West
Side of Manhattan and Harlem, and between Grunewald
in affluent southwestern Berlin and the working-class district of Prenzlauer Berg in the northeast.

The habit of traversing boundaries, and the notion that

doing so could benefit the understanding, is rooted in Bonhoeffer's teenage years. A diary from his Italian journey of 1924 notes how one's preunderstanding of people and nations can be transformed in the actual encounter with them. Bonhoeffer's American friend Paul Lehmann drew attention to the same conviction when he remembered Bonhoeffer's "boundless curiosity about every new environment . . . [and his] capacity to see [himself] and the world from a perspective other than [his] own."[2]

*Does it view Bonhoeffer's decision to join the German political resistance in the light of his other commitments?* Understandably, Bonhoeffer's collaboration with those who conspired to assassinate Hitler is the thing for which many remember him. But this decision must be understood as the culmination of a path of resistance to the Nazi regime, not a repudiation of everything for which he previously stood.

Bonhoeffer hinted at active resistance as early as April 1933, when he wrote in "The Church and the Jewish Question" that there may be times when the church is called not only to bandage those who fall under the state's wheel but to stop the wheel itself. In Tegel prison a decade later, he answered a fellow prisoner's question about his participation in the conspiracy with this image: "If he, as a pastor, saw a drunken driver racing at high speed down the *Kurfürstendamm* [a major Berlin boulevard], he did not consider it his only or his main duty to bury the victims of the madman, or to comfort his relatives; it was more important to wrench the wheel out of the hands of the drunkard."[3] In this case the metaphorical wheel is different, but the emphasis on intervening to prevent the suffering of bystanders is the same. There is a continuity of conviction here that should not be overlooked.

*Does it overlook or minimize his shortcomings?* Because

the Nazi era offers us so few Christian heroes, Bonhoeffer is often held up as a sort of Protestant saint for the twentieth century. It has become common, for instance, to depict him as someone who overcame Christian anti-Judaism in both thought and action. While there is much to learn from Bonhoeffer in this regard, it is easy to place a halo on the man, to allow contemporary interfaith concerns to turn the portrait of a flawed human being into a religious icon.

*Does it try to make him "one of us" by translating his life and thought into a contemporary idiom?* Admittedly, when we turn to Bonhoeffer we want to know not only who he is but who he might become for us. Yet this natural concern can give rise to representations of Bonhoeffer that turn out to be little more than projections of our own concerns. Particularly when Bonhoeffer's moral authority is invoked in discussions of hotly contested issues such as abortion and violence, we risk uncritical appropriations of his legacy.

## The Call to Radical Christianity

Having posed these questions in hopes of establishing the outlines of a genuine Bonhoeffer, we can fill out the picture with a few broad strokes of our own. Without doubt Bonhoeffer's meaning today will be tied to the uncompromising version of Christian discipleship he forged in the crucible of Nazi persecution. If Bonhoeffer had confined his following of Christ to what he calls in *Ethics* "the sanctuary of a private virtuousness,"[4] he might have enjoyed a relatively secure existence. Even if he had limited his resistance to the sphere of church politics, he would probably have avoided government persecution. But before the Nazis came to power Bonhoeffer recognized that obedience to Christ might well require suffering in and for the

world. "We should not be surprised," he preached in 1932, "if times return for our church, too, when the blood of martyrs will be called for."[5]

Thus, long before his execution, Bonhoeffer glimpsed the martyrdom that would mark the climax of his path of discipleship. In our fascination with heroes who remain strong in the moment of ultimate testing, it is easy to forget that many personal sacrifices preceded the spilling of Bonhoeffer's blood. Among the things Bonhoeffer was called upon to surrender were his professional prospects. Before 1933 he was on course for a promising academic career; after 1933 this promise faded with each decision he made. From university lecturer in Berlin to pastor of an émigré community in London to director of an illegal seminary to assistant minister in rural Pomerania, Bonhoeffer trod what for a young man of his ambition and talent was a path of profound humility. We see in Bonhoeffer's career, in fact, a movement from the center to the margins of society that counters our assumptions about the trajectory of a gifted life. In entering the conspiracy, Bonhoeffer slid even further into obscurity, renouncing "command, applause and the backing of general opinion" and forfeiting his reputation among those who assumed he had sold out to the Nazis.[6]

Another sacrifice required of Bonhoeffer along the path to martyrdom was the loss of a permanent home. From 1937 when he left Finkenwalde for the collective pastorates, Bonhoeffer was without the secure residence most of us take for granted as a staple of existence. In 1939 when he was offered refuge in America, Bonhoeffer decided to return to Germany to endure the coming crisis with his brethren. It would be difficult to fault Bonhoeffer had he remained in America, pursued an academic career, started a family, and lived into old age. But while morally defensible, this path would have been an evasion of the sacrifices to which he believed the Christian is called. Discipleship, Bonhoeffer teaches us, is defined by faithfulness not only in the final moments of one's life but in the multitude of moments that constitute it.

Bonhoeffer once described his life as "nomadic" and himself as a "sojourner" who dreamed of "a more settled existence with all the rights that normally go with one's 'rank' and age."[7] These were the physical and psychological costs of Bonhoeffer's nonconformity, of his refusal to submit to a state-controlled church. He bore them fully conscious of the fact that resistance to this church would make it impossible for him to enjoy a regular ministry, a parsonage, a salary, and a pension. These threats had a chilling effect on many of his fellow "confessors," leading them to declare loyalty to the National Socialist government and/or seek legalization from the *Volkskirche*.

As Eberhard Bethge concludes, beginning with Bonhoeffer's repudiation of the pastoral privileges offered by

the racist "people's church" of the German Christians, Bonhoeffer's life was "a constant fight to overcome the dangerously privileged character of the Christian religion; in his decision to take up theology, his move from teaching to pastoral work, and then to 'becoming a man for his own times' in the conspiracy against Hitler."[8] As one who freely and consistently relinquished the privileges associated with being Christian in a "Christian culture," Bonhoeffer presents us with a profound challenge.

## Bonhoeffer as Teacher

In a final note on Bonhoeffer's legacy, we want to draw attention to an often overlooked aspect of his character—the gift and desire he had for teaching. Despite his short career as a university lecturer, there is much evidence that Bonhoeffer possessed qualities we associate with influential educators. These qualities were evident in his energetic devotion to the Barcelona Sunday school, his triumph over the ruffian confirmands in Berlin, the uncommon ways he related to university students, and his powerful impact on the Finkenwaldeans.

Bonhoeffer's ability to connect with young people at a level beyond the academic was quite unfamiliar to most of his German students. What was behind this ability? Was he a "born educator," as his friend Franz Hildebrandt put it? Was it his "kindness to the young people," as his supervisor

in Barcelona observed? Did he combine the roles of "father, pastor and neighbor"? Was it his personality—his warmheartedness and the way he "turned his gaze fully towards him to whom he was speaking"? Was it the "scholarly qualifications and pastoral passions that were united in Bonhoeffer," a combination Reinhold Niebuhr referred to as "sophisticated theology and simple piety"?[9]

Or perhaps it was something deeper than technique, personality, or piety—a conformity of word and deed that is as attractive as it is rare. "It is for such a life of one piece, such an example that a young person longs," writes Albrecht Schönherr, a resident of the House of Brethren at Finkenwalde. "Bonhoeffer had nothing of the discontinuity of modern man. . . . He willed what he thought."[10] This unique integrity between life and thought, reflection and action, belief and obedience had a deep impact on those who knew Bonhoeffer. It impacts many of us still.

# Notes

## 1. Life

1. Eberhard Bethge, *Dietrich Bonhoeffer: A Biography*, rev. and ed. Victoria J. Barnett (Minneapolis: Fortress Press, 2000), 36.
2. Dietrich Bonhoeffer, *The Young Bonhoeffer, 1918–1927*, vol. 9 of Dietrich Bonhoeffer Works (Minneapolis: Fortress Press, 2003), 113. In future this work will be cited as *DBWE*.
3. *DBWE* 9:177.
4. Bethge, *Dietrich Bonhoeffer*, 70.
5. Dietrich Bonhoeffer, *Barcelona, Berlin, New York 1928–1931*, vol. 10 of Dietrich Bonhoeffer Works (Minneapolis: Fortress Press, 2008), 205.
6. Karl Barth, *The Word of God and the Word of Man* (New York: Harper Torchbook, 1957), 196.
7. *DBWE* 10:353.
8. For a thorough discussion of Bonhoeffer's relationship to Barth, see Andreas Pangritz, *Karl Barth in the Theology of Dietrich Bonhoeffer* (Grand Rapids: Wm. B. Eerdmans, 2000).
9. Bethge, *Dietrich Bonhoeffer*, 182.
10. Dietrich Bonhoeffer, *London, 1933–1935,* vol. 13 of Dietrich Bonhoeffer Works (Minneapolis: Fortress Press, 2007), 39.
11. *DBWE* 10:196–97.
12. Bethge, *Dietrich Bonhoeffer*, 75.
13. Ibid., 100.
14. *DBWE* 10:172.
15. Bethge, *Dietrich Bonhoeffer*, 106.
16. Ibid., 111.

17. *DBWE* 10:358.
18. *DBWE* 10:233.
19. *DBWE* 10:201.
20. *DBWE* 10:265–66.
21. Bethge, *Dietrich Bonhoeffer*, 158.
22. *DBWE* 10:269.
23. This is the view of Reinhold Niebuhr, writing in 1946. Bethge, *Dietrich Bonhoeffer*, 165.
24. Ibid., 174.
25. Ibid., 204–5.
26. See Clifford Green, *Bonhoeffer: A Theology of Sociality* (Grand Rapids: Wm. B. Eerdmans, 1999).
27. Bethge, *Dietrich Bonhoeffer*, 173.
28. Ibid., 211.
29. Ibid., 226.
30. Ibid., 188, 209; *DBWE* 10:372.
31. Bethge, *Dietrich Bonhoeffer*, 252.
32. Ibid., 315.
33. Ibid., 167, 258.
34. Ibid., 260.
35. Dietrich Bonhoeffer, "The Church and the Jewish Question," in *No Rusty Swords: Letters, Lectures, and Notes, 1928–1936*, vol. 1 of *The Collected Works of Dietrich Bonhoeffer*, ed. Edwin H. Robertson (New York: Harper & Row, 1965), 225.
36. Bethge, *Dietrich Bonhoeffer*, 302.
37. Quoted in *No Rusty Swords*, 242.
38. Franz Hildebrandt, "An Oasis of Freedom," in *I Knew Dietrich Bonhoeffer*, ed. Wolf-Dieter Zimmerman and Ronald Gregor Smith (New York: Harper & Row, 1966), 39.
39. *DBWE* 13:23.
40. *DBWE* 13:104ff.
41. *DBWE* 13:127.
42. *DBWE* 13:103.
43. *DBWE* 13:56.
44. *DBWE* 13:192.

45. Bethge, *Dietrich Bonhoeffer*, 395.
46. Ibid., 388.
47. *No Rusty Swords*, 290–91.
48. Bethge, *Dietrich Bonhoeffer*, 389.
49. *DBWE* 13:152.
50. *DBWE* 13:225, 229.
51. *DBWE* 13:285.
52. Bethge, *Dietrich Bonhoeffer*, 466.
53. Ibid., 512.
54. Ibid., 520.
55. Ibid., 497.
56. Ibid., 584.
57. Ibid., 603.
58. Ibid., 616.
59. Wolfgang Gerlach, *"And the Witnesses Were Silent": The Confessing Church and the Persecution of the Jews* (Lincoln: University of Nebraska Press, 2000).
60. Bethge, *Dietrich Bonhoeffer*, 637.
61. Larry L. Rasmussen, in *Dietrich Bonhoeffer: Reality and Resistance* (1972; repr. Louisville, KY: Westminster John Knox Press, 2005), speaks of Bonhoeffer's "provisional pacifism," "selective conscientious objection," and "agonized participation" in the resistance. This book remains the best analysis of Bonhoeffer's attitudes on issues of war and peace.
62. Bethge, *Dietrich Bonhoeffer*, 655.
63. Dietrich Bonhoeffer, *Conspiracy and Imprisonment, 1940–1945,* vol. 16 of Dietrich Bonhoeffer Works (Minneapolis: Fortress Press, 2006), 63.
64. *DBWE* 16:71.
65. *DBWE* 16:181.
66. *DBWE* 16:75.
67. *DBWE* 16:407.
68. Bethge, *Dietrich Bonhoeffer*, 737.
69. Ibid., 837.
70. *DBWE* 16:424, 453.
71. Bethge, *Dietrich Bonhoeffer*, 820.

72. *DBWE* 16:604.
73. *DBWE* 16:436.
74. Bethge, *Dietrich Bonhoeffer*, 826.
75. Ibid., 851.
76. Edwin Robertson, ed., *Voices in the Night: The Prison Poems of Dietrich Bonhoeffer* (Grand Rapids: Zondervan, 1999), 45–46.
77. Ibid., 76.
78. Ibid., 123.
79. Fabian von Schlabrendorff, "In Prison with Dietrich Bonhoeffer," in Zimmerman and Smith, *I Knew Dietrich Bonhoeffer*, 230.
80. Quoted in Bethge, *Dietrich Bonhoeffer*, 920.
81. G. K. A. Bell, Bishop of Chichester, "The Church and the Resistance Movement," in Zimmerman and Smith, *I Knew Dietrich Bonhoeffer*, 209–10.
82. Quoted in Bethge, *Dietrich Bonhoeffer*, 928.

## 2. Christ Existing as Community

1. Dietrich Bonhoeffer, *Sanctorum Communio: A Dogmatic Inquiry into the Sociology of the Church*, vol. 1 of Dietrich Bonhoeffer Works (Minneapolis: Fortress Press, 1998), 21.
2. *DBWE* 1:52.
3. Ibid.
4. *DBWE* 1:49.
5. Ibid.; translation slightly altered.
6. Dietrich Bonhoeffer et al., *Life Together and Prayerbook of the Bible*, vol. 5 of Dietrich Bonhoeffer Works (Minneapolis: Fortress Press, 1996), 38.
7. *DBWE* 5:56.
8. Clifford Green, *Bonhoeffer: A Theology of Sociality* (Grand Rapids: Wm. B. Eerdmans, 1999), 37.
9. Charles Marsh, *Reclaiming Dietrich Bonhoeffer: The Promise of His Theology.* (New York: Oxford University Press, 1994), 93.
10. Ibid., 8.

11. David H. Jensen, *In the Company of Others: A Dialogical Christology* (Cleveland: Pilgrim Press, 2001), 143.
12. Bonhoeffer, *Letters and Papers from Prison*, 13–14.

### 3. Costly Grace

1. Dietrich Bonhoeffer, *Discipleship*, vol. 4 of Dietrich Bonhoeffer Works (Minneapolis: Fortress Press, 2001), 45.
2. Geffrey B. Kelley and John D. Godsey, "Editors' Introduction to the English Edition," in Bonhoeffer, *Discipleship*, 6.
3. *DBWE* 4:45.
4. *DBWE* 4:44.
5. *DBWE* 4:53.
6. Ibid.
7. *DBWE* 4:49.

### 4. *Stellvertretung* and Ethics as Formation

1. Rasmussen, *Dietrich Bonhoeffer*, 39.
2. See Green, editor's introduction to *Ethics*, vol. 6 of Dietrich Bonhoeffer Works (Minneapolis: Fortress Press, 2004), 6.
3. Dietrich Bonhoeffer, *Christ the Center* (New York: Harper & Row, 1966), 62.
4. Bonhoeffer, *Letters and Papers from Prison*, 5.
5. Quoted in *Bonhoeffer*, Journey Films, 2003.
6. *DBWE* 6:93.
7. *DBWE* 6:94–96.
8. Bonhoeffer, *Letters and Papers from Prison*, 6.
9. *DBWE* 6:58.
10. *DBWE* 6:133.

### 5. Religionless Christianity

1. Bonhoeffer, *Letters and Papers from Prison*, 280.
2. Ibid., 279.
3. Ibid. Ralf K. Wüstenberg, *A Theology of Life: Dietrich Bonhoeffer's Religionless Christianity* (Grand Rapids: Wm. B. Eerdmans Publishing Co., 1998), takes up the question of Bonhoeffer's conception of religion.

4. Bonhoeffer, *Letters and Papers from Prison*, 281–82.
5. Ibid., 282.
6. Ibid.
7. Ibid., 312; emphasis added.
8. Ibid., 325.
9. Ibid., 360.
10. Ibid., 361.
11. Ibid., 361–62.
12. Ibid., 369.
13. Ibid.
14. Ibid.
15. Ibid.
16. Ibid., 369–70.
17. Ibid., 370.
18. Ibid., 362.
19. Geffrey B. Kelly and F. Burton Nelson, *A Testament to Freedom: The Essential Writings of Dietrich Bonhoeffer* (San Francisco: HarperOne, 1995), 495.
20. Robertson, *Voices in the Night,* 53.
21. Ibid., 369.
22. John Matthews, *Anxious Souls Will Ask* (Grand Rapids: Wm. B. Eerdmans, 2006), 18.
23. Ibid.
24. Bonhoeffer, *Letters and Papers from Prison*, 279.
25. Matthews, *Anxious Souls Will Ask*, 18.
26. Bonhoeffer, *Letters and Papers from Prison*, 280.
27. Ibid., 381; emphasis added.
28. Kelly and Nelson, *Testament to Freedom,* 494–95.
29. Bonhoeffer, *Letters and Papers from Prison*, 382.
30. Ibid.; emphasis added.
31. Ibid., 369.
32. Ibid.

## 6. Legacy

1. See Stephen R. Haynes, *The Bonhoeffer Phenomenon: Portraits of a Protestant Saint* (Minneapolis: Fortress Press, 2004).

2. Quoted in Bethge, *Dietrich Bonhoeffer*, 155–56.
3. Otto Dudzus, "Arresting the Wheel," in Zimmerman and Smith, *I Knew Dietrich Bonhoeffer*, 82.
4. *DBWE* 6:80.
5. Sermon in June 1932 in the Kaiser Wilhelm Memorial Church, Berlin. See Bethge, *Dietrich Bonhoeffer*, 236.
6. Ibid., 794.
7. Ibid., 594.
8. Ibid., 620, 876.
9. Hildebrandt, "An Oasis of Freedom," 40; Fritz Olbricht, "Report of Pastor F. Olbricht in Barcelona on Vicar Dr. Dietrich Bonhoeffer," *DBWE* 10:172; Hans-Werner Jensen, "Life Together," in *I Knew Dietrich Bonhoeffer*, 152; Sabine Leibholz, "Childhood and Home," in *I Knew Dietrich Bonhoeffer*, 33; Wilhelm Ott, "Something Always Occurred to Him," in *I Knew Dietrich Bonhoeffer*, 132; and Reinhold Niebuhr, "To America and Back," in *I Knew Dietrich Bonhoeffer*, 165.
10. Albrecht Schönherr, "The Single-heartedness of the Provoked," in *I Knew Dietrich Bonhoeffer*, 126–28.

# For Further Reading

Bethge, Eberhard. *Dietrich Bonhoeffer: A Biography.* Revised and edited by Victoria J. Barnett. Philadelphia: Fortress, 2000.

Bethge, Renate, and Christian Gremmels, eds. *Bonhoeffer: A Life in Pictures.* Minneapolis: Fortress, 2006.

Bonhoeffer, Dietrich. *Dietrich Bonhoeffer Works,* 17 vols. Edited by Victoria Barnett. Minneapolis: Fortress Press, 1996–2006.

De Gruchy, John, ed. *The Cambridge Companion to Dietrich Bonhoeffer.* Cambridge Companions to Religion. Cambridge: Cambridge University Press, 1999.

Green, Clifford J. *Bonhoeffer: A Theology of Sociality.* Grand Rapids: W. B. Eerdmans, 1999.

Haynes, Stephen R. *The Bonhoeffer Phenomenon: Portraits of a Protestant Saint.* Minneapolis: Fortress, 2004.

Kelly, Geffrey B., and F. Burton Nelson, eds. *A Testament to Freedom: The Essential Writings of Dietrich Bonhoeffer.* San Francisco: HarperOne, 1995.

Matthews, John. *Anxious Souls Will Ask.* Grand Rapids: W. B. Eerdmans, 2006.

Pugh, Jeffrey. *Religionless Christianity: Dietrich Bonhoeffer in Troubled Times.* New York: T&T Clark, 2008.

Rasmussen, Larry L. *Dietrich Bonhoeffer: Reality and Resistance.* 1972; repr. Louisville, KY: Westminster John Knox Press, 2005.

Schliesser, Christine. *Everyone Who Acts Responsibly Becomes Guilty: Bonhoeffer's Concept of Accepting Guilt.* Louisville, KY: Westminster John Knox, 2008.

For Further Reading

Wind, Renate. *A Spoke in the Wheel: The Life of Dietrich Bonhoeffer*. London: SCM Press, 1991.

Wüstenberg, Ralf K. *A Theology of Life: Dietrich Bonhoeffer's Religionless Christianity*. Grand Rapids: W. B. Eerdmans, 1998.

# Index

Index

# Index

# Index

CPSIA information can be obtained at www.ICGtesting.com
Printed in the USA
LVOW080950081212

310459LV00001B/4/P